South West London
Edited by Michelle Afford

 Young **Writers**

First published in Great Britain in 2008 by:
Young Writers
Remus House
Coltsfoot Drive
Peterborough
PE2 9JX
Telephone: 01733 890066
Website: www.youngwriters.co.uk

SB ISBN 978-1 84431 642 7

Foreword

Young Writers was established in 1991 and has been passionately devoted to the promotion of reading and writing in children and young adults ever since. The quest continues today. Young Writers remains as committed to the nurturing of poetic and literary talent as ever.

This year's Young Writers competition has proven as vibrant and dynamic as ever and we are delighted to present a showcase of the best poetry from across the UK and in some cases overseas. Each poem has been selected from a wealth of *Little Laureates 2008* entries before ultimately being published in this, our seventeenth primary school poetry series.

Once again, we have been supremely impressed by the overall quality of the entries we have received. The imagination, energy and creativity which has gone into each young writer's entry made choosing the poems a challenging and often difficult but ultimately hugely rewarding task - the general high standard of the work submitted ensured this opportunity to bring their poetry to a larger appreciative audience.

We sincerely hope you are pleased with this final collection and that you will enjoy *Little Laureates 2008 South West London* for many years to come.

Contents

Thushani Rajakumar (10)   22
Ghous Ali (10)   22
Joshua Khan (11)   23
Romell Claxton (11)   23
Danial Ahmed (11)   24
Faith Ogundele (10)   24

Eaton House the Manor School

Maximilian Himpe (9)   25
Jack Johnston (9)   25
William Holy-Hasted (10)   26
Hugh Spaughton (9)   26
Xander Hepher (9)   27
Morgan Gaysford (10)   27
Boris Belsky (9)   28
Gus Strong (8)   28
James Beggs (9)   29
James Brocklebank-Fowler (10)   29
Mungo Fenwick (10)   30
Guy Boliston (9)   30
William Siebert (8)   31
Elliott Pearson (8)   31
Charles Fox (9)   32
Alex Spencer (9)   32
Ben Schlossman (9)   33
Ben Player (8)   33
Max Stolkin (8)   34
Nicholas Katzaros (10)   34
Robert Moyse (8)   35
James Maidment (8)   35
Milo Osborne Young (9)   36
Thomas Eden (9)   36
Sidney Clack (9)   37
Aage Noble (8)   38
Oleś Morris (9)   38
Piers Bellman (8)   39
Lysander Sandberg (8)   39
Gabriel Beagrie (8)   40
Hugo Leopold (8)   41

Finton House School

Georgia Lee (11)	42
India Bamber	42
Katie Weatherstone (11)	43
Clara Lindsay (9)	43
Katie Craig (11)	44
Cordelia Royds (9)	44
Alice Jackson Rogers (11)	45
Rose McMillan (9)	45
Henry Eveleigh (10)	46
Ava Howard (10)	46
Rosie Whitbread (10)	47
Olivia Manzoni (10)	47
Sophie Potter (10)	48
Serena Wright (11)	48
Lili Gold (10)	49
Holly Gash (7)	49
Sarah Bliss (11)	50
Sophie Elliott (8)	50
Arabella Koessler (11)	51
Clemmie Beale (8)	51
Lara Ouvaroff (11)	52
Cordelia Rawnsley (10)	53
Polly Sellors (10)	54
Georgia Westgate (10)	54
Lucy Browne-Swinburne	55
Grace Walker (10)	55
Annabel Hewitson (10)	56
Hanna Walker (8)	57
William Macneal (7)	57
Ilse Henderson (8)	57
Flora Clark (7)	58
Bella Gibbs (8)	58
Isobel Scarlett Radford (7)	59
Imogen Andrews (10)	59
Rosie Craig (8)	60
Celeste Morris (10)	60
Ebrina Koster (9)	61
Hattie Glendenning (10)	61
Madeleine Swift (9)	61
Francesca Hicks (10)	62

Emma Rosier (9)	62
Ned Lindsay (8)	62
Tom Ibbitson (7)	63
Ollie Binks (7)	63
Amba Bharti (8)	63
Billy Leach (9)	64
Elisabeth Plunkett (10)	64
Sam O'Keeffe (8)	65
Niamh Cahill (9)	65
Phoebe Westgate (8)	66
Lucy Hewitson (8)	66
Lily-Rose Morris-Zumin (8)	67
Georgia Greaves (8)	67
Ella Simeon (8)	67
Alice Slade (8)	68
Sam Dawson (7)	68
Ellie Hancox (7)	69
Edward Samuelson (8)	69
Louisa Burwood (7)	69
Maude Martel (8)	70
Adam Merlin West (7)	70
Jago Skelding (8)	70
Savannah Davies (8)	71
Lucy Porter (9)	71
Josie Braithwaite (9)	71
Tilly Roberts (8)	72
Florence Fox (8)	72
Sophie Hicks (8)	72
Eliza Broadbent (8)	73
Helen Davey (9)	73
Georgia Stopford (9)	73
Megan Mann	74
Sam Browne-Swinburne (7)	74
Olivia Greenwell (8)	75
Hamish Fraser (7)	75
Arthur Rigg (7)	76
Ruby Lyons (7)	76
Harry Kinnings (8)	76
Olivia Andrews (7)	77
Tilly Ponsonby (8)	77

Furzedown Primary School

Andrew Thompson (11) Neil Maisuria, Aaron Goedluck & Isaiah Rafael Spencer Watson	78
Bilal Alam Khan (10)	79
Milli Ahern, Tino Smillie & Francesca Brooks (11)	80
Morgan Roberts-Watson (9) & Mohammed Aboobakar (10)	81
Arianna Boyd-Allen & Sophie Baldwin (10)	82
Priyanka Patel & Georgia Grant-Anderson (11)	83
Daniel Gollop (10)	84
Jessica Ramsay (11)	85
Stephanie Carruthers (10)	86
Joel Cameron Best (10)	87
Chelsee Ryan (11)	88

Glenbrook Primary School

Jamayne Cassar (11) & Jannell Wilkie	89
Donte Knight	89
Jordayne Daley (7)	90
Zakiatu Seisay (7)	90
Matilda Handley (9)	91
Jade Curran (8)	91
Emma-Lisa Monahan (9)	92
Olaoluwa Olanrele (8)	92
Chantae Williams (9)	93
Breanna Baker (10)	93
Laura Kieu Anh Le (10)	94
Kaleigh Balanta-Avalos (8)	95
Chynah Nicholls-Planter (9)	95
Alexandra Jones (9)	96
Leah O'Connell (9)	96
Billy Bradan Hudson (9)	97
Leighanne Gabrielle Brown (9)	97
Lamrana Jalloh (9)	98
Michael Allen (9)	98
Dontai Stewart (8)	99
Christian Ogiugo (9)	99
Daniella Parreira (8)	100
Sundis Hassan (9)	100
Henry Elezi (8)	101
Jamal Brown (8)	101
Jay Payne (9)	102

Shaftesbury Park Primary School

Stanford Primary School

The Poems

Soulja Boy Tow

I am the music maker,
I am the rhyme,
I am the rhythm,
The melody and time.

The beautiful sound of the electric guitar
Filling up the dance floor
Everyone dancing on the stage
Some people walk out the door.

The hard sound of the drum
Called a gong
Which banged in my ears
For so long.

The magical sound of the flute
Filled my ears with joy
Because it sounded
Like a hoot.

The wind sound from the shape of a semicircle
Is actually the harp
I bought it from the shop today
But it sounds so sharp.

The long sound of an instrument
Called a chime
It goes on for so long
It takes up all the time.

I am the music maker
I am the rhyme
I am the rhythm
The melody and time.

Sebastian Bolton (9)
Bonneville Primary School

Soulja Boy Rap

I am the music maker
I am the rhyme
I am the rhythm
The melody and time

The beautiful sound of a cello
Sounds very mellow
The sound of a xylophone
Sounds like someone having a go.

The electric guitar
You can hear from afar
The triangle
Sounds as quiet as a star.

I like the drum
Because it's loud
I like the steel drum
When I played it I was proud.

I want a violin
So it can go *ping*
I want a triangle
Because I like the ding.

Liam King (9)
Bonneville Primary School

Untitled

There was an old man called Sam,
He had a friend called Pam,
For dinner they would eat ham,
For tea they would eat lamb,
That old Sam and Pam.

Ellie Harper (8)
Bonneville Primary School

The Music Maker

I am the music maker
I am the rhyme
I am the rhythm
The melody and time

The sound of a saxophone
Makes me jump up and down
And when I hear the music
I always turn around

The sound of a violin
Makes me jump up and down
And when I hear the music
I always have a frown

The sound of a drum
Beating like a heart out of breath
And when I hear it beat
I dance with my feet.

The sound of a drum set
Beating and beating
And when I hear the drum set
I always start eating.

Najma (9)
Bonneville Primary School

Columbian Lady

There was once a young lady
Who always sat on a daisy
A truck came up
She thought she was in luck
Because she'd just had a baby.

Winessia Williams (8)
Bonneville Primary School

Soulja Boy Rap

I am the music maker,
I am the rhyme,
I am the rhythm,
The melody and time.

The beautiful sound of the electric guitar,
Filling up the dance floor,
Everyone is dancing on the stage,
When rude people just walk out the door.

The sun is so bright,
It fills the world with light,
The clouds are so fluffy,
I am going to name my dog Duffy.

The harp is so nice,
The mice want to have spice,
When I hit my head,
I need to go to bed.

Every day my teacher
Takes the register in French,
In our school I sit on the friendship bench.

Santino Ofori (9)
Bonneville Primary School

The Man Who Drank Beer

There was an old man who drank beer,
Whose behaviour was very queer,
He sat on a pin,
Then itched his chin,
And chased his wife with a spear.

Madeleine Butler (7)
Bonneville Primary School

The Music Maker

I am the music maker,
I am the rhyme,
I am the rhythm,
The melody and time.

The beautiful sound of a piano sounds quite mellow
The sound of the xylophone sounds like a cello.

I'm the beautiful sound of a drum
The sound of a trumpet
Makes me want to hum.

The lovely sound of a xylophone

The sound of a guitar
Makes me hungry for fritters.

I am the sound of a flute
Take me to the opera, I'll put on a suit.

The voice of a violin
The tune of the trombone
The wonderful sound of the cowbell
Makes me want to phone home.

Dominic Burrell (9)
Bonneville Primary School

Boat Kennings

Sea sailor
Wave bobber
Country traveller
People mover
Cargo carrier.

Ryan Scullion (8)
Bonneville Primary School

Music Maker

I am the music maker
I am the rhyme
I am the rhythm
The melody and time.

I'm the sound of a piano
Loud and sharp
I'm the squeaky sound of the violin
And the harp.

I am the latest hit
By Stevie Wonder
I control his dance moves
And his voice sounds like thunder.

I like rap music
Jazz, classic and pop
But opera is a real big flop!

I am the music maker
This is very true
When I hear a rap song
I think of you.

Kimone Johnson **(9)**
Bonneville Primary School

Untitled

There was a man, Carter was his name.
A famous archaeologist,
He found the tomb and rose to fame.
The only one to find Tut's tomb,
A curse forever.
Would he be doomed?

Keisha Sullivan **(9)**
Bonneville Primary School

The Music Girl

I am the music maker,
I am the rhyme,
I am the rhythm,
The melody and time.

I'm the sound of a piano,
The lovely melody it makes,
I'm the beautiful sound of a violin,
With the harmony it shakes.

I am the latest hit,
By the Jackson Five,
I control their dance moves
And control their minds.

I like rap music,
Classical, jazz and pop,
When I listen to disco music,
I feel like I want to drop.

I went out shopping,
But then I heard a lovely drum,
It came from an orchestra,
And then everybody started to hum.

I went out to my music class,
But then I heard a gong,
It sounded so good,
I even made it into a song.

I am the music maker,
I am the rhyme,
I am the rhythm,
The melody and time.

Nadine Manar (9)
Bonneville Primary School

Music Maker 24

I am the music maker
I am the rhyme
I am the rhythm
The melody and time.

I am the music maker
I like a bit of rock
When I turn on the TV
It always goes to pop.

I like playing the guitar
I also like the drum
I don't like the trumpet
But it does make me hum.

My favourite band is 'Police'
I nod my head to the beat
When I was good once
I saw them for a treat.

I am the music maker
I don't like the flute
I like the triangle
Cos it looks so cute

I am the music maker
I am the rhyme
I am the rhythm
The melody and time.

James Wadmore (9)
Bonneville Primary School

I Am The Music Maker

I am the music maker,
I love R'n'B,
I know my music facts,
All the way from A to Z.

I am the music maker,
I like a bit of pop,
When you turn on the TV,
It always turns to hip hop.

I am the music maker,
I wanna sing a song,
But when I sing it, sing,
'Cause the words come out all wrong.

I am the music maker,
I love to play a harp,
The only bad thing is,
The notes are much too sharp.

I am the music maker,
I hate the snare drum,
Although I can play it,
I'd prefer to hum!

I am the music maker,
I am the rhyme,
I am the rhythm,
The melody and time.

Ethan Hayter (9)
Bonneville Primary School

Too Much Noise!

I am the sound of a saxophone.
I am the sound of a gong.
It goes *bang*.
When I get strong.

When the drum crashes,
I go mad.
When the chimes are whining,
I get bad.

When I play, the flute goes *hoot,*
It makes a sound.
When I play my flute,
The sound is loud.

The harp is wonderful.
It is sharper than a razor.
I can play it loudly,
But it hurts my fingers.

Aneeka Katri (9)
Bonneville Primary School

That Silly Old Lady

There was an old lady from London
That took a Tube to the Dungeons
She got stuck in the loo
She was having a poo
That silly old lady from London.

Shyla Sultan (8)
Bonneville Primary School

The Music Maker

I am the music maker
I am the rhyme
I am the rhythm
The melody and time.

I'm the sound of a piano
I'm the deep voice of a cello
I'm the beautiful sound of a violin
I'm the colour of yellow
I'm the latest hit by Stevie Wonder
I control his dance moves
And his voice sounds like thunder.

I like rap music, classical, jazz and pop
I am the music and I sound so sharp
I am the music maker, this is very true
I am the music maker and this is true.

Kevone Morrison (9)
Bonneville Primary School

Cat Kennings

Curtain scratcher
Mouse catcher
Milk drinker
Fish eater
Purr maker
Fly chaser.

Tyra Badiel (8)
Bonneville Primary School

Dog Kennings

Stick catcher
Bottom licker
Meat eater
Cat chaser
Bark maker
Tongue sticker
Fur leaver
Fetch player
Ball fetcher
Floor sleeper
Sofa biter
Paper chewer.

Lucy Zokou (8)
Bonneville Primary School

New Girl

I stood on my own
No one to play with
Looked at people running, playing, screaming.
But no one to play with me.
People were saying horrid things
But I pretended I didn't care
But I did.
I felt like crying.
I behaved like I didn't care
But I did.
Tears came out of my eyes.

You think it doesn't matter
But it does!

Mahnoor Tariq (10)
Broadwater Primary School

Dance Of Death

People are whooping like mad
To see a tortured bear dance,
My body,
Dry as the Sahara Desert,
The chain up my nose and mouth,
With menacing pain!
My owner shows no mercy,
He doesn't care
About my excruciating pain.
My fur,
Colourless and grey,
My owner gets paid
To see me, a tortured bear, dance.
My bloody, red-stained nose,
Drooping,
It feels as if the world is against me,
My mum was shot,
I wish I could join her,
My shabby hair,
Falling out,
Dancing for hours under a flaming sun,
It's like Hell!
When I was free,
I wasn't suffering
Then they took me away,
Not even feeding me,
Making me weak,
Also making me exasperated!

Please help!

Alex Sliska (11)
Broadwater Primary School

Tortured For Entertainment

I once had a home,
I was happy, strong with my family.
Joy, happiness was there.

Care, love - all that went,
When the bipeds captured me
As some sort of prisoner.
I was muzzled.
My teeth were forced out permanently
As I was dragged along.
My life now is cold,
My future is dim.
My nose is sore and painful,
Oozing with blood
As I'm trying to perform
For those cold-hearted people.
I have to work or my master will beat me.

Then I hear a voice, he says . . .
'I was once captivated by cruel bipeds,
I will let your soul free.'

Suddenly I am free . . .
Free from those cruel bipeds.

So I dance like never before -
It is the dance of freedom!

Ira Samuel Bielby (10)
Broadwater Primary School

The Dancing Bear

Soiled coat,
Hair jagged,
Upon the stage I shriek and stumble,
Muzzle tight,
Cold and lonely,
No one cares.

Audience cheering,
I must perform,
Waiting for the music,
I do my act.

Exhausted body,
Bloody nose,
Taken to my cage,
Locked up again.

This cruel world,
Is my life,
Nothing compared to the one before,
When I used to run freely,
Doing what I wanted,
Eating when I felt hungry,
My coat all white and glossy,
Leaving me happy . . .

This feeling; gone forever!

Natasha Yong (11)
Broadwater Primary School

Lonely

I was having a lot of fun,
With all my mates,
When they just left without a word.

I felt so alone, I didn't know what to do,
I just walked around the playground
Then I followed them,
To see what they would do,
I asked them a question
And they ignored me.

They blanked me
Again and again,
Till I felt microscopic.
They said I had problems,
But I didn't listen,
I ignored them.

Shanai Barnes (10)
Broadwater Primary School

Dancing Bear

I was pulled by my demanding master,
I had to dance for hours.

I finally had a break but with no food
And no water, I was dying of thirst.

I remember when I was free,
I would go by the river and hunt down my food.

I would follow my mother,
Until they took her away from me.

Wherever I go, the tormenting pain
Of my mother's death still haunts me.

Mitchell Kellar (11)
Broadwater Primary School

Dancing Me

Tourists smiling
Taking pictures
And I'm in chains, unhappy.
They're watching me
But what they don't see
Is the torture they're putting me through.
Just the feeling I have
Like 10,000 daggers through my already broken heart
And shattered dreams.
Finished the dance,
Now we're back to the start.
No!
I won't, this is the last dance.
I wrap the rusty chains around my neck,
Now I'm free . . .

I can dance with my mother!

Louis Moore (11)
Broadwater Primary School

Rejected

Dejected and gloomy,
Cheerless and dreary,
Unhappy and troubled,
Doleful and disgruntled.

My footsteps as loud as my heartbeat,
To them I am as quiet as a mouse,
Watching them hop and skip,
I want to go back to my house.

Watching them play hopscotch,
Like ballerinas across the playground,
Making me feel so lost,
I just can bear their happy sounds.

Davina Rehal (10)
Broadwater Primary School

Things You Can Find In A Doctor's Pocket

A drawer full of injection needles,
A van full of patient's measles.

A wardrobe full of stethoscopes,
A dying man's hopes.

One hundred patients waiting,
1,000 magazines dating.

A baby about to be born,
A mother shouting at Doctor Dorn.

A long white coat,
The size of a boat.

Evisa Terziu (10)
Broadwater Primary School

Bear

Some people came rushing through,
Shot my mum and took me away,
They took me to a place I never knew,
But now I do.
I don't get anything to eat or drink,
The skinny old man makes me dance,
If I don't he hits me really hard with a long wooden stick.
He pulls me angrily up with a fat long string tied to my nose.
You don't know how I suffer,
My blanket used to be a cosy nest,
But now it's just a dirty dry bush.
I don't know what to do!

Shahella Shabnam Ahmad (10)
Broadwater Primary School

Cruelty To A Little Cub

The little frail cub,
Was chained and muzzled up,
What cruelty they would do,
Poor little bear locked in a rusty cage.

Not even knowing what was happening,
I was so sad and full of rage,
The crowd cheered . . .
'Dance again!'

He was scruffy like a rug,
His eyes were frail,
He was in a lot of pain . . .

I wish he could survive!

Gwynyth De Vera (10)
Broadwater Primary School

Sometimes

Sometimes
I have a party
But no one comes,
Sometimes
I speak but no one listens,
Sometimes
I don't care if others stare
Because . . .
Sometimes
I stare back!

Hassan Hamid (10)
Broadwater Primary School

The Dancing Bear

I awoke,
I was being pulled by my nose.
I screeched with pain.
I stood up,
Wobbling with anguish,
Pain and dread,
Slowly and aggressively,
Pain flowing through my furry body.
'Ow!'
There went my furry skin being poked.
I used to be free,
Filled with happiness.
Now I danced for vicious beings,
My fur was stiff and dry,
I was weak,
I knew this was what my life would be like . . .
Dancing
Forever.

Hamza Minhas (10)
Broadwater Primary School

Left Out

I felt horrid inside when I asked a person to play
And the answer was 'No!'
I had mad feelings about him.
I wish I could have done it back
But I let him off.
I got angry inside and asked my mum what I should do.
She said, 'Try and help him understand what it's like being left
                                                                out all alone.
So I told him what it was like.
So he let me play but he forgot what I told him.

Arif Afaq Elahi (11)
Broadwater Primary School

Dancing Bear

Hair glued together,
Coat all rough,
Agony travelling through my dirty body.

Humans smiling,
While a tearful, miserable face I have.

Wild, was massive,
And I was contented,
Eating healthily,
But they took me away,
Cheers now follow me wherever I go.

With humans I feel scared,
My mother has been shot,
And I was taken away,
My heart has run away from me,
Leaving me to suffer.

Humans are cold-hearted,
When they hurt animals!

Ummah Ullah (11)
Broadwater Primary School

Dancing Bear

Mouth muzzled, can't open my mouth
Mum! Dad!
Come and kill these people
Bring some rescue people
Roaring and screaming for freedom
Every day, every morning
They make me dance
They put a stick in my nose!

Khumair Ahmed Junjua (10)
Broadwater Primary School

Wishes

The river's wish is to be related to the moon.
But, the river is not related to the moon
    That wish did not come true.
However, the river is proud because the moon reflects
                                    on the river at night.

The stem's wish is to smell lovely like the flower.
But, the stem doesn't smell lovely like the flower.
    That wish did not come true.
However, the stem is proud because at least it holds up the flower.

Just like these, not every wish comes true, so
Live with happiness; with what you have.
Live with joy of what you achieve.

Thushani Rajakumar (10)
Broadwater Primary School

Agony

I feel petrified, with nothing to eat, nothing to drink.
Barefoot I dance,
With a chain through my nose,
The brutal man is beating me,
With his thick stick.
I am dying from thirst and hunger.
In the wild I was healthy and strong,
Full of minerals and water.
Now I lie in the burning sun,
Weak as a cat.
In a chain . . .
I die of grief!

Ghous Ali (10)
Broadwater Primary School

Liverpool FC

Liverpool are the best I do not doubt,
With the lanky long legs of Peter Crouch,
Steven Gerrard leading us to victories,
With all of the players using their abilities.
Pepe Reina is our saviour,
Whilst our young midfielder is Lucas Leiva.
With Alonso scoring from the halfway line,
The future with this club looks just divine.
The acceleration of Ryan Babel,
Enables Fernando Torres to score against our rivals,
The heart of our defence is Carragher and Hyypia,
With the powerful left foot of John Arne Riise.
Our new American owners bring in the cash
To buy new players like Iker Casillas,
The subs on the bench chant with the crowd,
'You'll never walk alone', it's heard out loud.

Joshua Khan (11)
Broadwater Primary School

Left Out

They call me 'fat boy',
(I'm so disgraced).
They taunt me, they peer,
They poke and they jeer.
I'm desolate, I'm enraged,
They act like I need a cage!

I'm distressed, I'm dismal,
Downhearted from these people.
Why do they do this?
It's not right at all!

Romell Claxton (11)
Broadwater Primary School

Left Behind

I'm left behind when I want to play,
I'm left behind when I want to go on holiday,
I'm left behind when I want to sing and dance,
I'm left behind because of the way I dress,
I'm left behind because of my language and the way I talk,
I'm left behind because of my race,
I'm left behind because of my age,
I'm left behind because of my shape and size,
I'm left behind because of my disabilities,
I'm left behind because of my knowledge,
I'm left behind because of the way I am.

I'm alone in the world, like a lost child,
I have no one with me,
I'm joyless and I have no friends,
I wish I were somebody else,
I'm cheerless and it's all my fault,
I'm lonely,
I'm on my own,
I'm left behind.

Danial Ahmed (11)
Broadwater Primary School

Horrible Life

My young life was turned into a terrible one.
I felt like one million daggers hit my heart,
It felt like a dragon burnt my fur.

I suddenly cried for health and rest
But all I got was death!

My work was all a shame
For I was a dancing bear,
I rather felt like running
Through the peaceful forest.

But all I could do was suffer miserably.

Faith Ogundele (10)
Broadwater Primary School

When Uncle Came To Stay

When Uncle came to stay
He told us he needed to pay
For the beer when he got drunk
And for kicking the zoo's old skunk.

My uncle's not a positive man
Definitely when he cooks (and breaks the pan).
He sits around and growls
Also when Ronaldo does bad fouls.

He breaks our old quills,
And forgets his sleeping pills,
So he sleepwalks in the night
And paints our red walls white.

He watches boring opera shows
And crows back to the crows.
My uncle isn't so nice to have to stay
But at least he doesn't eat the horse's hay!

Maximilian Himpe (9)
Eaton House the Manor School

Humans

The world is one big planet,
There are lots of different species,
There is one type of species that is dumb but clever,
This species has got hes and shes.

This species are humans,
They are like an ape,
Except they are a bit clever,
And they do not misuse tape.

Humans are starting wars,
About a silly thing,
I think we all agree
To stop cutting down trees!

Jack Johnston (9)
Eaton House the Manor School

My Mum Is Going Shopping

My mum is going shopping
In the shop next door,
I think it is a ghastly thing,
Because it's such a bore.

My mum is going shopping,
(It's like doing a chore),
When she takes me with her,
I feel I want to snore.

My mum is going shopping,
Every day more and more,
I think it is silly,
Because she bought an apple core!

My mum is going shopping,
It's worse than scrubbing the floor,
And one night she came back and said,
'I bought a bear's claw!'

So now you know
How I feel,
When Mum says,
'I'm going out to buy some veal!'

William Holy-Hasted (10)
Eaton House the Manor School

The Adventurous Doctor Who

The adventurous Doctor Who,
Had nothing else to do,
So he went into the past,
Saw a Dalek at last,
And put him straight into the zoo.

Hugh Spaughton (9)
Eaton House the Manor School

Holiday Madness

Last summer I went to Portugal,
This time I went to France,
The things that happened this holiday,
Will really make you laugh!

As we arrived in France, we landed near a hose,
I walked down the plane steps,
Tripped up and nearly broke my nose!
When we got to the house,
I stepped out of the car,
I saw a mouse and, trying not to be scared, I said,
'Let's go to the bar!'

Next morning I woke up and found I had lumbago,
I thought to myself,
Hopefully, I can still go to Gambado!'

When I was better, I went in the swimming pool,
There I broke my back, and now I wonder
If holidays are better than school!

Xander Hepher (9)
Eaton House the Manor School

My Teacher Is A Tramp

My teacher is a tramp
And sits there with her lamp
She makes all her money
Then spends it on some honey
I see her in the shops
Trying to sell stuff and buy her daily chops
She gets kicked out of M&S
Then throws up on her dirty dress
She needs to buy a cheaper lamp
Then save up and stop being a tramp!

Morgan Gaysford (10)
Eaton House the Manor School

Jelly Belly Custard

Jelly belly custard,
Green slop pie,
All mixed together in a dead dog's eye,
Put it in a sandwich,
Eat it up quick,
And drink it all down,
With a cup of cold sick.

Put a snake in the oven,
And put some bones on your plate,
It will feed about a dozen,
But savour the taste,
Till it's all too late.

Ring all your friends,
Invite them round,
Don't feed them too much
Or they'll all grow round,
But when they pop,
Call a cop,
If they find out who did it,
You'll be busted!

But don't blame me if you're so disgusted!

Boris Belsky (9)
Eaton House the Manor School

Lovely Limerick

There once was a boy called Gus
Who lived on a double-decker bus
It didn't have a door
Which was a bit of a chore
But he didn't really make a fuss.

Gus Strong (8)
Eaton House the Manor School

I Don't Know What To Do Today

I don't know what to do today,
Go to the cinema,
Steal a bumper car,
Go on a plane,
Buy a candy cane?

I don't know what to do today,
Go to Santa's grotto,
Go and write a motto,
Fall off a swing,
Go and see the king?

I don't know what to do today,
Buy a chain,
Pull a horse's mane,
Light a fire,
Touch a phone wire,
Climb Everest,
Be the cleverest?

James Beggs (9)
Eaton House the Manor School

The Day Of The Geography Test

It was the day of the geography test,
I said to my mum, 'But I have such a cold.'
I faked a cough, I faked a sneeze,
But she did not give me any ease.
Finally the guns silenced, my mum gave in
But she said it was a sin.

I chilled and relaxed all day,
But I did not know how much I would pay.
The next day everyone said, 'Yeah,
Now you can have the test today.'
I felt sad and mumbled, 'I will never miss another day.'

James Brocklebank-Fowler (10)
Eaton House the Manor School

Time

Time passes in a flash,
You haven't noticed that.
Seconds going, when coming to a minute,
While minutes go to hours in such a rush.
Clocks go on ticking all the time,
You will notice that time never stops.
Something will happen every minute,
As time always will go on.

The good things in life tick away,
Too quick to stay and play.
When we have to go back to work,
We would like to go back to the past of fun times.
We all like to dream back in time,
But we don't have the time.
The only time we are allowed to dream,
Is when we go to bed.
Where we will have little hours to dream,
In a comfy bed.

Mungo Fenwick (10)
Eaton House the Manor School

Ink Pens Are Cool

Ink pens are cool,
You can swap them at school,
You can get some with codes,
You can even get some that make you quick.

Lamies, Parkers, Pilots and Biros,
My favourite one is definitely a Lamy,
Because you can get them gold,
You can get them silver,
But I have to say the best are the ones that are transparent.

Ink pens may be cool,
But you have to remember to bring them to school,
Or you will have to use that annoying tool.

Guy Boliston (9)
Eaton House the Manor School

Winter Poem

In wintertime I can see
Snowballs chasing after me
I see white snow
And Santa shouting, 'Ho, ho, ho!'

In wintertime I can hear
The wind howling against my ear
Across the fields church bells ring
And happy choir boys carol-sing.

Icy fingers, freezing toes
Chilly ears and a runny nose
Time for getting warm and snug
By the fire on the rug.

William Siebert (8)
Eaton House the Manor School

Winter Poem

In wintertime
The sounds I hear . . .
The snow beneath my feet
I can hear the sound of heat
In the blaze of the fire
Then I go much higher.

In wintertime
I can smell
Delicious marshmallows
Fresh, cold air
From the breeze.

In wintertime
I can see
Snow killing leaves
From the trees
In wintertime

Elliott Pearson (8)
Eaton House the Manor School

Teacher Tantrum

Today in maths I said, 'Ten plus one is two!'
And then my teacher said,
'I wish I was at home today, lying in my bed.'
But then I decided to eat my glue.

My teacher threw a tantrum on the floor,
And when we thought to pull her hair,
She yelled, 'This isn't fair.'
After that she spoke no more, 'cause we kicked her out the door.

We swore in the lockers,
We played in the playground,
And made a very noisy sound,
Then the headmaster came and yelled,
'Drop the bats, drop the balls, you've all gone bonkers.'

Detention had come,
We threw our balls and swung our bats,
But best of all we killed some cats,
Then the headmaster began to run . . .

And threw a tantrum on the floor!

Charles Fox (9)
Eaton House the Manor School

A Young Kangaroo

There was an old man from Renfrew,
Who purchased a young kangaroo.
It bounced up the street,
Under everyone's feet,
So he sold it to Edinburgh Zoo.

Alex Spencer (9)
Eaton House the Manor School

Losing My Locker Key

I hate losing my locker key,
My dad always shouts at me,
He hates it when I lose my key,
My teacher has the spare one.

Inside my locker,
Is my lunch fee,
My teacher does not care,
If I lose my key,
But she gives the spare one to me.

If I lose the spare key,
My dad has a
Plan C key,
Just for me.

Together I have three
Locker keys,
When I find it,
I jump with glee,
Then I can pay
My lunch fee!

Ben Schlossman (9)
Eaton House the Manor School

The Woman From Ealing

There was once a woman from Ealing,
Who had a peculiar feeling,
She let out a shout,
And it sort of turned out,
That her feet were stuck to the ceiling!

Ben Player (8)
Eaton House the Manor School

Season Poem

In wintertime I can see
Children playing in the white powdery snow,
People opening presents at Christmas time,
People laughing, eating and lighting up tree lights.

In wintertime I can taste and touch
Cherry and raisin pudding
Ice-cold snow that's just fallen down from the sky
Delicious and smothering gravy.

In wintertime
I can smell
Smoke from the log fires
Something delicious about to be eaten
Scrumptious raisin pudding
And some sweet slimy custard.

Max Stolkin (8)
Eaton House the Manor School

The Clean Loo

Flush, mosh, swoosh, mush the toilet goes,
When it sits there all day long with its wonderful pose,
Soggy loo paper on the floor,
When you step on it, it splashes the door.

Clean water inside,
Out comes a boy with a wet patch by his side.
The rusty loo seat makes you faint,
But you have to pray to a saint
That you'll be OK!

Not even one bar of soap is anywhere near that loo,
A naughty boy always chucks up his disgusting stew.
The toilet is battered and old,
And the white on that toilet is just plain bold.

Nicholas Katzaros (10)
Eaton House the Manor School

Winter Poem

In wintertime I can hear
Christmas carols in the church
Noisy fireworks at New Year
Freezing wind whooshing in my ears
People splattering snowballs on the common.

In wintertime I can smell
Pine needles on the Christmas tree
The table and the Advent candle.

In wintertime I can see
Snowflakes on the cars
Fog and frost on the common
Bare trees with no leaves
Fat turkeys on the table.

In wintertime I can touch
Cold, cold snow
And slippery ice
Tickly tinsel on the Christmas tree.

In wintertime I can taste
Roast turkey and potatoes
Snowflakes falling on my tongue
Hot food in a dish.

Robert Moyse (8)
Eaton House the Manor School

Zombie

I was wallowing in my bathroom
When a zombie arrived from the gloom
So I squirted shampoo
And showered him with glue
And he dragged me to my doom.

James Maidment (8)
Eaton House the Manor School

Winter Poem

In wintertime
I can hear
The snow crunching under people's feet
Walking up and down the street,
The laughter of children having a snowball fight,
Carol singers outside someone's door at night.

In wintertime
I can see
Large Christmas trees in the gardens,
Snow falling down from the sky,
Smoke coming out from people's chimneys,
People rushing to the shops.

In wintertime
I can smell
Christmas dinner in the oven,
The blazing of the candles in the room,
The berries and holly on the window,
The smell of red wine and champagne.

Milo Osborne Young (9)
Eaton House the Manor School

The Man From Dubai

There once was a man from Dubai
Who strangely said goodbye
'I shall see you soon
Maybe at noon,'
Said that strange man from Dubai.

Thomas Eden (9)
Eaton House the Manor School

My Teacher Likes To Play The Guitar

My teacher likes to play the guitar
Comes during all the lessons
He also comes round during gym sessions
He would play it anywhere, he would play it any place
If he could, he would play it on holiday

The day before half term, he pulled out his guitar
He went to a golf match and jammed over there
When the golfer was about to be on par

My teacher loved watching television
So he made his decision
My teacher let us watch a movie
While he was in the classroom trying to play a piece called 'Groovy'

My teacher likes to play the guitar
He bought a cool electric guitar, I was amazed
I couldn't see, I was at the back,
I pushed through everyone and gazed
At the amazing sight of my teacher's guitar, bright
In all of the lights
He grabbed a microphone and started to sing
But then I heard the school bell ring
We were all sad we had to go home, it was the weekend
We got on the bus, the doors swung open,
My teacher jumped on as we went round the bend

I got back home and jumped in my swimming pool
Then realised most teachers can be cool!

Sidney Clack (9)
Eaton House the Manor School

In The Summertime

In the summertime
I can see
All the birds tweeting in a tree
With all the lambs seemingly bleating at me
And soon the seagulls scavenging for sand crabs
I can see the sun in the deep blue sea.

In the summertime
I can hear
The trees all swaying
With the small donkeys braying
Then the small squirrel scurrying into the bushes
In the garden town.

In the summertime
I can feel
I love to stroke the smooth grass
And I love the feel of the smooth green leaves
I love to watch the flowers
And the days seem to last for hours.

Aage Noble (8)
Eaton House the Manor School

My Brother Once Visited A Zoo

My brother once visited a zoo,
And all of a sudden went *atishoo!*
The giraffes took fright,
And started to nip and bite,
Oh what a terrible hullabaloo!

Oleś Morris (9)
Eaton House the Manor School

Spring

In springtime
I can hear
Birds screeching in my ear
Or children splashing in puddles
And me getting into a muddle.

In springtime
I can see
Buds growing on the tree
When the sun hits bluebells, daffodils
And tulips they glow
Whilst children have a rugby ball to throw.

In springtime
I can touch and smell
A flower such as the bluebell
Which is found in the wood
Smell and feel fresh and good.

Piers Bellman (8)
Eaton House the Manor School

Season Poem

When I peak out of my crystal-clear window
I can see a rainbow
Like a garden full of shapes and colours
I can see bears clawing at the buzzing bees
To get the sticky honey.

In the springtime
I can smell pollen from freshly picked daffodils
The smell of green lush grass hits me like a burning comet.

At the end of spring I can see
Spring turning into summer
How the cold turns into heat
And rain turns into sunshine.

Lysander Sandberg (8)
Eaton House the Manor School

Spring Poem

In springtime
I can see
Colourful leaves on the brown trees
Blossoms growing under the beaming sun
Bees buzzing around
Sucking honey from the flowers

In springtime
I can hear
Birds singing with joy
Cockerels calling as day is dawning
Sheep bleating in the meadow of fresh green grass
Eggshells cracking as ducklings are born.

In springtime
I can taste
Granny's hot-cross buns
Covered in butter slipping into my tum
Easter eggs found covered in paint
Shared with my sister, the little saint!

Gabriel Beagrie (8)
Eaton House the Manor School

Winter Poem

In the winter
I can see:

White snow shining in the winter sun
Water under a layer of ice made by the wintry nights
Empty trees swinging through the winter sky
Children making snowmen in the streets

In winter
I can feel:

A cold breeze on my face
My hands stiffening every second
Getting tired from skiing
The snow under my feet

In winter
I can smell:

Fresh cold breeze in the air
Smoke coming from the chimneys
Food being cooked in the houses
Pines falling from the trees

Hugo Leopold (8)
Eaton House the Manor School

The Shadow Monster

I am closed up tight under my cover
with my back against the wall,
edging further away from the side of the bed
for I know there is something tall
lying directly beneath my head.

I hear a heavy breathing
and a huge shadow
is sprawling across my wall.
A dark blanket is covering me
and I feel so small.

I am shutting my eyes
and listening to myself breathe
curling up in a ball,
imagining I am somewhere else.
In, out, in, out, imagining I am somewhere else.

Georgia Lee (11)
Finton House School

Grizzly Bear

I walked quickly through the forest,
Looking fiercely all around,
I saw something colossal and scary,
And I heard a mysterious sound.

The creature came closer
Then it roared at me,
Its sharp teeth were gleaming,
I think it wanted its tea!

I was getting scared,
Its claws dived into my flesh
After the raging bear swallowed me,
The creature was refreshed.

India Bamber
Finton House School

Koala

I was hiking through a forest,
Feeling the cool breeze,
I heard a strange sound
And a rustling in the trees.

Then it came out of its hiding place,
And it looked at me,
Its beady eyes staring,
It was grey and furry.

Its colossal ears were listening
To the sound of the night,
Its sharp claws were showing,
That's when I got a fright.

It crept closer to me,
There was such a display,
Its sharp teeth were showing
And then I ran away!

Katie Weatherstone (11)
Finton House School

Phinpasok

I dive through the sea
I am a wave crashing across the world
I am the blue ripple floating in the diamonds of the sea
I am the front crawl of an Olympic swimmer
In the deepest depths
I am the blue food colouring dripping in the white water
I dart through the dark sea
I play where nobody can touch my silky scales
I'd hate to be caught because . . .
I am a miracle!

Clara Lindsay (9)
Finton House School

There Is A Creature Under My Bed!

There is a creature under my bed,
With dozens of spots all brown and red.
It swaps my books and borrows my toys,
Jumps on my sofa and makes a loud noise.

It has the teeth of a shark,
And a noise like a *bark.*
When it goes for a snack,
It brings me some back.

It's big and hairy with small green eyes,
With fur that's buried with nits and flies.
It picks me up when I fall,
Comes into the garden when I play ball.

My friend moved away, whose name was Ben,
The creature arrived exactly then.
And though one friendship came to an end,
Another started with a big hairy friend.

Katie Craig (11)
Finton House School

The Lion

I am the one that has sharp claws,
Nobody can roar like me,
I am the king, there is no prince,
So get away from me here.
I am hungry and so are you
I might just eat you, and you, and you!
I have a mane that you'll want to touch
But if you do, I'll eat you up.
I control you, but you don't control me,
So I'm taking you back into the dark with me.

Cordelia Royds (9)
Finton House School

When The Lights Go Off

It slithers like a snake,
While I lie awake.
Rummaging around my bed,
Filling me with dread.

Under the covers it dives,
With jaws as sharp as knives.
I pull away the duvet,
But the creature remains alive.

Rough skin swallows it,
Beady yellow eyes sting its face.
It seems like a long race,
Trying to make space.

Suddenly it freezes,
Closes its mouth of shame.
The lights are on,
And it's for me to blame.

I pull away the covers,
To check what's lurking beneath.
And to my surprise, it's nothing,
Just my old ted 'Beaf'.

Alice Jackson Rogers (11)
Finton House School

Limju

I am hungry,
I am bloodthirsty,
I'm coming tonight.
When the clock strikes twelve,
The knight will fall dead
And all will be unwell;
Another innocent person will go to Hell,
So don't get in my way.

Rose McMillan (9)
Finton House School

Cushebur

I am a Cushebur -
I am like a horse.
I am like a sheep.
I am like a tiger.
I am like a leopard.
But my personality is like no other living creature -
I do not need to eat.
I do not need to drink.
I move by attaching myself to the ground
And throwing myself a mile away.
I am an endangered species
So don't hurt me.
I question all actions.
Why should I not?
Smile at me and I frown.
Frown at me and I smile.
I am the brains behind NASA.
That is me.

Henry Eveleigh (10)
Finton House School

The Furflop!

This creature I'm going to tell you about
Is furry with a pink pig-like snout
This creature is delightful: gorgeous and fluffy
Though at times, it can be pretty scruffy!

Its abilities are kind of queer
I know you're thinking of your brothers but this is nowhere near!
It jumps around completely mad, like a newborn turtle
And when it talks, it screams like Moaning Myrtle.

When sleeping it snores and it sounds like a lullaby
But when it meets new people it is *very* shy
This creature is the one I love dearly
And I think it's loving me back . . . well nearly!

Ava Howard (10)
Finton House School

An Intrepid Journey

I slowly slithered up the cellar stairs,
Wearing darkness like a cloak.
Being careful not to wake a soul,
I finally reached the kitchen.

Peering inside I saw my prey,
The blood steak was waiting for me,
Thoughts of juicy meat,
Filled my head,
One bite and I would be in Heaven!

On my way back down the stairs,
I heard a creaking noise,
Coming from the bottom step.
Suddenly a black hooded figure,
Was right in front of me.

Shivers ran through my body,
Suddenly I saw a glint of shiny metal,
Getting closer and closer by the second!

Rosie Whitbread (10)
Finton House School

The Adorable Little Dragon

Flames, the adorable reptile,
Has extremely sharp claws,
He likes to devour raw meat,
Which he murders with his powerful paws.

His blistering skin is scaly and red,
And he has huge pricked ears on the top of his head.
Flames doesn't eat with a mouth but a jaw,
If he tries to bite you, he'll only manage a gnaw!

With four short legs and a spiky tail,
He tries to be scary but always fails!
You'll love him to bits, he'll become your friend,
He'll stay with you forever; until the very end.

Olivia Manzoni (10)
Finton House School

Fireflies

When I was younger I would settle on a tree stump,
Waiting for my grandfather to arrive;
When he finally came we were able to catch fireflies.

They appeared to be golden stars hanging in the night.
When one landed on my arm, I couldn't help but giggle -
Their mini legs moved swiftly up my arm.

When the firefly dived off, a buzzing noise began
And I knew that the touch the firefly gave,
Was a touch of love and light.

They had huge, sparkling, black holes for eyes,
And legs so skinny they looked like twigs,
Their minute antennae stuck out of their heads
And swayed in the wind.

Then my grandfather wrapped his arms around my tiny body,
And I realised that the warm air hitting my face,
Was his heart touching mine.

Sophie Potter (10)
Finton House School

The Poisonous Spiker

The Poisonous Spiker can soar through the sky,
He's electric blue with silver stripes.
He has poisonous spears from his forehead to his back,
And webbed hands and feet with tiny claws.
The Poisonous Spiker is a small eating scavenger,
He has night vision and can be heard for miles,
And has a little muzzle so he can smell his prey.
He can exhale fire but cannot be burnt,
The Poisonous Spiker has seriously sharp teeth,
And if you are touched by his poisonous spikes,
Then you will drop dead to the ground!

Serena Wright (11)
Finton House School

The Lowik

Lowik is the name of my cute and cuddly creature
So I have been told by a Finton House teacher.

It's cuter than a teddy bear
And it's got lots of red, fluffy hair.

It smells rather odd
It comes from Planet Smod.

It has huge eyes
That sees things flying by.

It squeaks like a mouse
It echoes through my house.

It has a very lengthy tail
Its speed is the opposite of a snail.

It's very chatty
Not at all scatty.

It's very calm
Sitting in my palm.

It's very petite
With its little dragon feet.

Lili Gold (10)
Finton House School

The Keypiberry

The Keypiberry is big and fat
With a pink tongue a mile *long*.
Feathery wings, big black eyes and a little tail.
It flies around in the black of night
Swooshing and gliding, glistening as well.

Its favourite thing is to show off
To friends and mates how it catches its prey.
It snatches its prey with its sharp, pointy claws
And stuffs it into its purple mouth.

Holly Gash (7)
Finton House School

The Snake

Coiled around an old oak
Eyes gleaming with deadly flame
He lies
In suspended silence.

Descending from his small abode
He sights a helpless rodent.
Suddenly his slick olive body
Becomes a hunter.

The scaled athlete (with an air of finality)
Slithers over the bed of needles.
The rodent, aware of danger, pricks his ears
But is it too late?

Closer and closer
Comes the angel of death

Indigo eyes full of venom
He strikes,

And the move is made.
The rodent suppresses
One last gasp
And lies still.

Sarah Bliss (11)
Finton House School

Creatures

I am a whale swimming round the bay.
I am fast like a lightning flash,
I have something secret to say -
Creeping down underground,
Closing down in my mind,
All hope of being found.

Sophie Elliott (8)
Finton House School

The Creature In The Loft

Quickly I gallop,
Down the stairs.
Desperate for air,
I stop.
Look up at the door.
Hear snoring.

I move closer,
Tentatively pushing it.
Looking inside,
I see,
Cupboards, shelves and drawers,
Food!

Wondering what to take,
I move towards the crisps.
Then hearing a whisper,
I charge towards the door,
And escape.

Galloping back up the stairs,
I race towards my safe haven.

Arabella Koessler (11)
Finton House School

Creatures

Eyes as yellow as the sun,
Lips as red as blood,
A voice as deep as the ocean,
Ears as big as mangoes,
A body as thin as a single piece of card,
I can see him coming towards me -
I find myself falling to the ground.

Clemmie Beale (8)
Finton House School

The Creature

Down deep in a violet loch
Where the wave of the water
Click-clocks
Over the long stringy seaweed
Where fishes by their millions feed

Do not be put off by his crimson eyes
His silent smile, his air of surprise
Lacoober is his name and watching is his, oh,
So deadly game!

Under the rocks, seaweed too
Stands a lair belonging to you-know-who
The water down there is ebony-black
Nothing will be hurrying back

The world around him
Turned around him
Lived around him
Until . . . that dreadful day when
The last of his kind
Died away

Morning awoke but the
Lacoober not with it
His eyes stayed closed
Till he reached
His last living limit

And the he just disappeared . . .
His existence with him!

Lara Ouvaroff (11)
Finton House School

The Magical Creature Full Of Friends

In the depths of my slumber,
I see the same man,
He shows me the creature,
Then looks at the sand.

The curve of the body,
And the pointed fins,
The colour of the creature,
Its silver skin.

'The magical place,
The sparkle in the land,
Please follow me,
I do understand.

I know how you feel
I know you're sad,
But if you believe in yourself,
It won't be so bad.'

I turned back to school,
But stopped and had to stare,
My dreams had come true,
People do actually care.

I slowly turned back,
But the creature was gone,
I wanted to say thank you,
And tell him all along I was wrong!

Cordelia Rawnsley (10)
Finton House School

The Creature

They spin with silken yarn,
A fragile thread across the barn.
Weaving and working all night long,
Breakable but so strong.

Some are small and some are vast,
Some are slow and others fast.
They have no nest,
And they barely rest.

Some are completely harmless,
Others cause disaster, even death.
They often appear then disappear,
Surprising us all and causing fear.

Polly Sellors (10)
Finton House School

The Creature

Long legs gripping tight,
Holding on with all his might,
Swinging from the emerald tree,
He's in the jungle and he's free.

They love to swing on branches high,
They're land animals, they cannot fly,
They're not tall, they're not small,
They're the cheekiest animal of them all.

Some are slow and some are fast,
They climb trees as high as masts,
They're members of the ape family,
They're the smallest one, the monkey.

Georgia Westgate (10)
Finton House School

The Creature

Each and every one
Of you should know
That there's something in
Your living room!

Not candlesticks
Or bronze antiques
But a creature
With an ugly form!

It might be big
Or it might be small
It might cough
Grunt or drool!

What does it eat?
How does it speak?
I don't know
But it's a *Tadakepeek!*

Its life is short
But don't be distraught
Because it's nearly
Extinct from your sight!

Lucy Browne-Swinburne
Finton House School

The Phinpanade

I am the hurt Phinpanade
I am the one who has injured a fin
I am the one who is sinking to the bottom of the sea
I am the one who has been defeated by the Phinpasok
In the shimmering sea
I am the one who has a dagger in his heart
So beware the Phinpanade!

Grace Walker (10)
Finton House School

Mowtickle

Little one crouching in the wood,
No one but you could
Be so timid, shy or scared.
Watching for danger you see a nut,
Look around and pick it up,
Examine it and hug it to you when . . .
Watch out,
Look behind,
The Plemagdi is there!
You run and run,
But not for fun,
You must get to your secret weapon.
You turn around,
Turn bright red,
Fire growing out of your head.
Slowly you become a giant.
You're even bigger than *Plemagdi!*
You stamp your foot,
Caloo, Calay!
The *Plemagdi* is dead today.
Little one crouching in the wood,
No one but you could
Be so timid, shy or scared,
But wait!
You're none of these but,
Mowtickle,
Terror of the wood!

Annabel Hewitson (10)
Finton House School

Moondonkey

I am a friend of the lovely donkey
Who can leap over the sea,
He can fly to the moon,
And he looks like a beautiful, beautiful, lovely donkey.
He has taken me to an amazing world of brightness,
Then he gave me a ride in the sea,
But now, he is the moondonkey.

Hanna Walker (8)
Finton House School

My Creature Ponguinprin

His big, fiery eyes glowing
His fuzzy fluffy tummy shimmering
His narrow bubbly back prickling.
His hairy, powerful legs swift
His round, giant face blowing.
His pointing, chunky nose honking.

William Macneal (7)
Finton House School

Firebird

I am the flicker of the fire,
Going in every direction,
In a flash you see me coming,
Running, oh, so cunning,
Shiny and red will gaze your eye,
I am your firebird coming by.

Ilse Henderson (8)
Finton House School

Chepinice

A Chepinice has hair as hard as wood.
Eyes as big as emeralds.
Teeth as black as coal,
But they never fall out.

Skin rough and scaly.
Wings cold and wicked.
They flutter higher and higher
To kill its prey.
Wings with icicles
To freeze its prey.

It screeches as loud
As five children screaming.
Fingers zap through the walls.
Lasers cut through anything.
Nails as sharp as needles.

Flora Clark (7)
Finton House School

Creatures

Eyes the colour of green grass,
Lips as red as poisoned apples,
Mouth as smooth as a slug,
Eyes as big as peaches,
Back as crawly as cacti,
Claws as long as a lion's,
Legs as big as an elephant's,
Body as big as a house,
Oh no! He's coming out of the mist towards me,
Running, my heart starts to race -
It melts so fast now it begins to flutter.

Bella Gibbs (8)
Finton House School

Yasogi

Teeth magic and mouldy
Black and crumbly.
Fingers wrinkled and dirty.
Wings silky and golden.

Hair spiky and knotty.
Eyes wide and innocent, also wise.
Skin flexible to bounce off
Any sharp daggers or swords.

Breath like a gutter that kills people.
Eyes giving strange looks to people.
Ears able to hear guns
1,000,000,000 miles away!

Using his crinkly, old fingers
To rub his claws,
He cackles like a thousand
Witches screaming.

Isobel Scarlett Radford (7)
Finton House School

Chozebpip

I'm lone, quiet and slow,
In the summer sun that is never hot,
I sit on rocks that are never hard,
I'm reaching for a star I can never reach for,
I'm the Chozebpip in the summer.

I'm leaning on a tree with no trunk,
I'm sleeping in a bed with no mattress,
I'm the Chozebpip at rest.

I'm walking through snow that isn't cold but hot,
I'm running on a beach with no sand,
I'm the Chozebpip on the move.

Imogen Andrews (10)
Finton House School

Freshalium

Freshalium, Freshalium
Gentle but frightening,
Still and breathtaking.

Freshalium, Freshalium
This bold creature with webbed feet
Makes you shrivel up inside.

Freshalium, Freshalium
He glides through the water
Like a glimmering fish.

Freshalium, Freshalium
Why are your eyes
So bloodshot and sad?

Rosie Craig (8)
Finton House School

The Klelemrabb

With kangaroo-like paws I pounce at 100mph
Like a racing stallion in the wild
I stop in the sight of the sparkly sunset
I look around myself thinking *the air is quite mild*
I go to the field to rest my head
Maybe I'll have a good sleep,
The leader of the pouncing says.
I run in the morning
While the sun is still dawning
As the sunset comes down again
I go and say my prayers to them.
The next morning I have a warning
That I will never pounce again.

Celeste Morris (10)
Finton House School

The Koxielp

I know the way to the end of the world,
I am like an ox fighting in the darkest of nights,
My teeth are extraordinary, as sharp as swords,
I sleep in the caves, my snore is deafening,
I cry so loud that the sun shakes,
I have no souls that know I live,
I am all alone in the deepest cave,
I get so hungry I can make it rain,
I can eat the Earth in one gulp.

Ebrina Koster (9)
Finton House School

The Bubtaca

I am the sea that never flows,
I am the wind that never blows,
I am the window that never opens,
I am the sun that never burns,
I am the party with no guests,
I am the clown that never laughs,
I am the book that is never read,
I am the Bubtaca!

Hattie Glendenning (10)
Finton House School

The Starwichcobb

I am the hope and the light of the world,
Yet I am trapped and cannot get out
My heart is the treasure chest of feelings,
But my cry for help is deafened,
My voice is the wind in the trees,
So, come my saviour, come.

Madeleine Swift (9)
Finton House School

The Leirpaco

His body is like lightning dashing to the ground
And when he wants food he is an eagle starting to pound.
His body is like icebergs, starting to crack
And he belongs to a big pack.
He has a voice like a pink pelican going *quack!*
And like a crocodile going *tak!*
He prays every night saying, 'O' Mightiness,
Put us back to normal, please!'

Francesca Hicks (10)
Finton House School

The Shigarit

I am the sea growling in the wind,
I am the racing car zooming away,
I am the stop sign not letting anyone pass
Without me eating them,
I am a fierce sumo wrestler.

I am also a rabbit jumping with joy,
I am the calm summer's sea sending you to sleep;
Sending you to sleep,
But actually there is only one thing I am;
I am the *Shigarit!*

Emma Rosier (9)
Finton House School

Vinbarco

Eyes like a red ruby.
Teeth like gold daggers.
Wings like flames in the air.
Hair glistening like a snake's scales.
Breath like volcanoes spitting flames.
Claws as sharp as knives ready to grab its prey.

Ned Lindsay (8)
Finton House School

The Idletrumts

The Idletrumts has . . .
Silver teeth glowing
Grey feet stamping
Huge, slimy fingers crunching
Hard skin burning
Messy hair crawling
His sharp toenails are unbreakable.

Tom Ibbitson (7)
Finton House School

The Dodrurite

The Dodrurite has . . .
Bright eyes beaming
Scaly skin shining
Spiky wings flying
Ugly fingers scratching
Sharp teeth eating
Stinky breath blowing
Long hair bristling
His dirty, hard head is like a rock.

Ollie Binks (7)
Finton House School

The Bitogite

The Bitogite has . . .
Bright white teeth eating
Bright blue eyes staring around
Smooth silky skin breathing
Soft tail wagging
Fluffy ears twitching.

Amba Bharti (8)
Finton House School

The Cacrocoag

Crawling, sneaking up behind you.
As it strikes you feel cold and drop to the ground,
Croaking, you breathe your last breath.
Ready you must be because he is,
Or if you are ready there is no chance
'Cause the Cacrocoags are coming.
On the coldest night in August when the clock strikes twelve,
A breeze pushes the trees, and then they appear.
Great fear on this cold night, because they are here;
They're coming.

Billy Leach (9)
Finton House School

The Gookasee

I am the controller, which commands everything
I am as fast as lightning and as wise and as clever as an owl
I make you fight, or be friendly
I see into the future and I know what you look like
I can haunt you
I can see what you see
My eyes are as big as three marbles put together
A body as big as yours
If you want to see me walk and walk
I live far away.

Elisabeth Plunkett (10)
Finton House School

The Puppeelzza

The Puppeelzza is very hairy,
But he is not scary.
Skin as smooth as glass,
Eyes as evil as pirates.

Fingers as jagged as a stone
At the bottom of the sea.
Wings as gold
As the sun in Dubai.

Hair as fluffy as my dog Alfie.
Teeth as sharp as a brick on a house.
Skin as hot as fire
And a soul as big as eternity.

Sam O'Keeffe (8)
Finton House School

Femoeam

Life is running through his veins
Tensing as he runs,
Makes a lunge every time
As he fires,

Darkness closing in on him
But beckons it away,
And fights a cry every day
Femoeam, come to me.

Niamh Cahill (9)
Finton House School

Doonadeimal

My wings are extraordinary but fascinating, I see.
They do not fly, they crinkle like me.
My teeth are black.
My hair is green.
I am not very beautiful at all, I see.

My teeth are mouldy, they are, they are.
My skin is so scaly, slippery and slimy.
My eyes are great, glistening all day.
They see things a mile away.

My fingers are dirty.
My eyes are flirty.
My hair is knotty, but shiny it is.
It swishes like clothes on a washing line
On a windy day.

But inside my body
There is a heart all kind,
All kind and happy like yours!

Phoebe Westgate (8)
Finton House School

My Creature Angocola

Glittering brave eyes glowing in the moonlight.
Vast, long wings flapping through the air.
Shining lifting-up hooves gleaming in the air.
Big, soft head nodding in the clouds.

Strong white teeth shining in the light.
Long, narrow tail wiggling through the soft blanket of clouds,
Searching in the air for the rainbow.
Carrying others as the sun sets.
It glows in the night.

Lucy Hewitson (8)
Finton House School

My Creature Arpypas

My creature is so chubby his friends all run away.
His tail is huge and bendy.
His wing is as sharp as a pointed piece of hay.
His big feet smell like a rubbish bin.
His pointy, wet fin is flapping so fast in the wind.
His ugly face is staring right at me.
His scaly skin is rough and green.
I am very scared!

Lily-Rose Morris-Zumin (8)
Finton House School

Roobuiltia

Like a kangaroo I am,
Pouncing through all the mountains,
No hope of being liked,
Ruining all their fountains,
I don't mean to ruin all,
But every time my mum has to call,
I have to be there on time.

Georgia Greaves (8)
Finton House School

My Creature Magiberrypup

Her juicy red face is glossy,
Her soft fluffy body is shining,
Her white hard teeth are biting
Her brown soft ears are listening.

Her soft white feet are slippery,
Her soft tail is gleaming,
Her blue eyes are shining.

Ella Simeon (8)
Finton House School

The Bogey Monster

I look into the night,
I see the moonlight shining on an awful sight.
I don't know what it is.
It looks like something that whizzes,
It's slimy, not at all shiny,
It has a nose like a honker.
It's the bogey monster!

I run and run then climb up a tree,
It comes galloping after me,
It stops then leaps,
I fall down in a big heap,
I stay there with my eyes closed,
For a whole week!

Alice Slade (8)
Finton House School

My Ballanco

He has a big wobbling stomach,
A dark, winking eye,
Vast sharp feet,
His menacing legs are wiggling,
His pointy long teeth are sparkling,
His feet are moving again,
His scary head is coming,
He is flapping, now he's off.

He's wagging his tail,
Flapping his wings,
His eyes are going beady and red,
His feet are burning bright!

Sam Dawson (7)
Finton House School

My Creature Dooteneets

Her fluffy, sparkly eyes are twinkling,
Her black cute head is nodding,
Her white, shimmering teeth are flashing in the dark,
Her pink shiny body is moving.

Her furry yellow paws are walking,
Orange leathery legs are jumping,
She adores playing with her blue stripy tail!

Ellie Hancox (7)
Finton House School

My Creature Muzzasqui

His gloomy red eyes are staring.
Those blade-like teeth are eating.
He has fast, long legs ready to pounce.
Just look at that rough, scaly skin
Getting harder every second.

Don't forget his huge, strong head is really hard to crack!

Edward Samuelson (8)
Finton House School

My Creature Angaleke

His face as chubby as ever.
His beady eyes looking at me.
A sharp fin flapping on his head.
Four teeth ready to tear apart some meat!

His body, sloppy and melting in the hot summer sun.
A mouth as big as a human.
Running at fifty miles an hour.
I am terrified of the Angaleke!

Louisa Burwood (7)
Finton House School

The Nyoshta

Its skin is a dark green.
Its hair is long and curly.
Eyes are wide and sharp.
Teeth pointy and gnashing its prey
And wings sharp and gleaming.

Eyes glistening like volcanoes searching for prey.
Hair twisting like snakes wrapping around its prey.
Skin shooting out green hair and spots.
Teeth ready for gnashing food
And wings like daggers ready to kill its prey.

Maude Martel (8)
Finton House School

My Creature Owlpasger

His sharp, blade-like claws scratching.
His spiky back shining in the morning.
His sharp teeth sharpening.

His bullet-fast body going faster.
His beady blue eyes getting hotter, glowing.
His multicoloured tail flashing.
His spiky hair sharpening.

Adam Merlin West (7)
Finton House School

My Creature Tonotco

His bent horns were charging up with shiny white plugs.
His blade-like teeth were grinding.
His huge sharp claws were holding onto his big wet meat.

He had rusty broken nails.
His rusty, wriggling and fidgeting legs needed oil.
He had lots of writing paper and wings on his back.

Jago Skelding (8)
Finton House School

Prisoner

Eyes like a demon looking for its prey,
Skin of a serpent who's coming today,
He has the wink of lightning,
And a brightening smile,
Feet the size of a mouse,
Favourite food is woodlouse!
Arms like a stick,
Legs so thick,
But what about the heart?
It is so dark!

Savannah Davies (8)
Finton House School

Donoesta

Eyes like glinting emeralds
Claws like pearly white bones
Skin as soft as a leopard's skin
Breath like a small hurricane.

Inside I have a small broken heart
Full of things that I don't want.

I wish I could just find a friend
Out of the eerie darkness.

Lucy Porter (9)
Finton House School

Snake

S lithering through the sand,
N ibbling on a mouse
A ttacking in a house,
K illing every prey it meets,
E verybody fears it!

Josie Braithwaite (9)
Finton House School

Tiger

On the prowl,
As fast as lightning,
Hunting in the jungle for food.

Newborn cubs play fighting,
Sleeping deep in a high tree.

Black and orange fur,
Made into a rug!

This is the tiger!

Tilly Roberts (8)
Finton House School

The Flaming Tiger

The leaping tiger with eyes bright.
Its soft coat like velvet with flaming stripes.
The tiger growls at sunlight and its roar pierces your ears.
It moves slowly with its long, thin, graceful tail burning bright.
But be careful, the mysterious tiger can smell you everywhere!

Florence Fox (8)
Finton House School

The Cheeky Monkey

M onkey is a cheeky one, he climbs everywhere,
O ver the trees, through the branches and elsewhere,
N aughty sometimes, likes laughing about stories,
K eeps swiping people's hats,
E very day he swings and swings,
Y es, he has to go!

Sophie Hicks (8)
Finton House School

Rillaturzeb

I am a gorilla swinging in the trees,
I am a turtle swimming in the sea,
I am a zebra running in the sun,

I have dark blue eyes,
I have spotty, soft fur,
I have a brown long tail
And I also have the biggest heart of all,
So always remember me - the Rillaturzeb!

Eliza Broadbent (8)
Finton House School

Bubatgo

I am a tree swaying in the wind,
I am the waves splashing on the cliffs,
I am the voice that's never been heard
But my breath is just like fire,
I am the thunder going *bang, bang, bang!*
I am a spider spinning its web
I am a tiger pouncing on its prey
Because I can take you away.

Helen Davey (9)
Finton House School

Tiger

T iger, a stripy jumper,
I ts face like a car's bumper,
G ets its energy from fresh meat,
E very roar troubles prey's fast-moving feet,
R oars like a drummer's beat.

Georgia Stopford (9)
Finton House School

Puppdoogoo

Big black fur glistening.
Sparkly eyes, hairy feet and pointy teeth.
He went to the shop and everyone screamed.
'He's big, he's ugly,' they said.
So he went back home, all sad and blue.
'What shall I do?' he said.

Next day he went for a walk
And again they screamed
All except Mr Andy Ant.
He was small and Puppdoogoo was big,
But he was not afraid!
They became best friends
And walked off together happily!

Megan Mann
Finton House School

The Ullcotite

The Ullcotite has . . .
Bulging red eyes staring
Huge hands stretching
Sparkling skin spiking
Bony feet clicking
Rough hair swishing
Horrid breath stinking
A glittery mouth munching
Disgraceful teeth clashing.

Sam Browne-Swinburne (7)
Finton House School

The Ziggypizog

The Ziggypizog has . . .
Red bulging eyes blinking
Rotten, muddy, leafy teeth clashing
Slimy skin eating
Sharp, stinky breath breathing
A hairy nose killing
A black shadow following
Huge ears calling
A poisonous mouth swaying
His tail is as straight as a stick.

Olivia Greenwell (8)
Finton House School

The Maphantbe

The Maphantbe has . . .
Huge, gurgling eyes looking
A slithering tongue licking
Sharp, long teeth chattering
Smelly, stinky breath breathing
Scaly, shimmering skin shining
Long, light legs leaning
A big, bold body bulging
Huge, jumpy hair wriggling
A tangly, tingly tail tossing
His claws are as sharp as razors
And can kill a man as he likes.

Hamish Fraser (7)
Finton House School

The Richittlekit

The Richittlekit has . . .
Scaly, bony wings flapping
Deep blue, ice-cold skin breathing
A dangerous tail whipping
Sharp, icy teeth chewing
Ruby-red eyes hunting
Cold, powerful breath blowing
Sharp, iceberg claws scratching
This is . . .
The Ice Dragon!

Arthur Rigg (7)
Finton House School

The Horsparlate

The Horsparlate has . . .
Fleshy feet stumbling
Floppy, furry ears clattering
Chocolate-brown skin shivering
Knotty hair strangling
Mean blue eyes glowing
And skin as shiny and sparkly as shells.

Ruby Lyons (7)
Finton House School

The Omchocoda

The Omchocoda has . . .
Green wings spinning
Floppy ears hearing
Purple skin gleaming
A slimy tongue licking his prey
A delicate body bouncing
His body is like a purple pepper.

Harry Kinnings (8)
Finton House School

Chocoumpda

Chocoumpda has . . .
A big, snotty nose snoring
Long, floppy ears drooping
Rubbery, wrinkly skin wobbling
A curly, squiggly tail twitching
Chocolatey, sugary breath stinking
A slimy, long tongue licking
Stubborn short feet walking
Long, wiggly arms grabbing
Huge green eyes looking
He loves to eat chocolate
He stuffs it all in.

Olivia Andrews (7)
Finton House School

The Iteuppywof

The Iteuppywof has . . .
Jagged, crooked teeth snapping
Glistening blue eyes staring
Almighty wings flapping
Teeth-grinning mouth dribbling
Dagger-sharp claws scratching
Burning-fire breath fizzling
White-as-snow hair bouncing
Powerful body pouncing
Big, silky ears flapping
His legs are like pounding tigers.

Tilly Ponsonby (8)
Finton House School

Operation Evacuation

Now it's autumn,
The trees are shedding their leaves,
It reminds me
Of my lovely memories.

I remember my dad saying,
I was on a secret operation,
A secret mission he called it,
Operation evacuation.

I live in the countryside,
Cos World War II has just begun,
I used to live in a nice house
With my dad and mum.

In my city,
Gary was my friend, my chum,
Now, I am lonely,
Sad and glum.

I am always thinking
Of my mum and dad,
When I was with them,
I was just a little lad.

I do not know where
My future is going,
Even now, as I watch
The flowers growing.

Now the grass
Is swaying in the wind,
It feels like my life
Has just been binned.

Andrew Thompson (11) Neil Maisuria,
Aaron Goedluck & Isaiah Rafael Spencer Watson
Furzedown Primary School

My Gran

I loved my gran,
She loved me back,
She loved everyone and everyone loved her,
But why did she have to die?

I loved my gran.
Why did she have to die?

Soup was her favourite dish,
She ate it with me,
We both liked sitting together,
But why did she have to die?

I loved my gran.
Why did she have to die?

She loved me a lot,
She spoiled me rotten,
I loved her enormously,
But why did she have to die?

I loved my gran.
Why did she have to die?

She died too early,
I really loved her,
But why did she have to die?

I loved my gran.
Why did she have to die?

I'll always remember my gran,
Her memories will stay in my heart,
But why did she have to die?

I loved my gran.
Why did she have to die?

Bilal Alam Khan (10)
Furzedown Primary School

Train Ride

Sitting on the train, thought I was in trouble
Miss Green called me over on the double

I went to her and said, 'Yes, Miss Green
All this war is just too mean.'

'I know how you feel, I went through the same
This whole war is just too insane.'

'Thanks Miss Green,' I said, satisfied
But I cannot hide.

I cannot wait till this war is over
I thought as the train pulled in at Dover.

I'm very anxious for my mum's letter
That's coming in the post.

I think about my family throughout the night
I think about my mum all the time.

Milli Ahern, Tino Smillie & Francesca Brooks (11)
Furzedown Primary School

Evacuee

I work on the farm every day
It's really boring because all you hear is *neigh*

I wake up in the morning and I take a bath
I do cover up, don't be daft

I don't work on the farm all day
Of course I go to school, nah, you don't say

I got in a fight with a German kid
I was scared and frightened, therefore I hid

When I see my brother I get all happs
But when I see my four sisters I just collapse

My host family isn't all bad
But when I think of my mum and dad I get really sad

My chores I have been given, some good, some bad
Oh no, the pigs need cleaning!

Morgan Roberts-Watson (9) & Mohammed Aboobakar (10)
Furzedown Primary School

Evacuee Poem

I am sad
Am I going mad?
I'm alone
I want to go home,
I'm working on a farm
And living in a barn,
I now feel joyful
But at the same time thoughtful,
They let me keep my cat
But it has to sleep on the doorstep mat,
I'm hungry but I cannot eat
And when I go to bed I cannot sleep,
I am so lonely
My host family are always moany,
I go to the barn and get some eggs
Then I put our clothes on the washing line with pegs,
I miss my dad and mum
And the host family are nuns.

Arianna Boyd-Allen & Sophie Baldwin (10)
Furzedown Primary School

The Evacuee

I'm in the kitchen sweeping the floor
And all I want is Mum to walk through the door;

All I wanted was to have some fun
But now I have ended up in this slum;

I miss my mum and my dad too
All I need is a hug from you;

I'm milking the cow on a hot summer's day
I take out the letter but she says, 'Put it away.'

I'm so lonely, so lonely and sad
All I want is for Mum to write, then I will be glad;

No one likes me, no one at all
All I ask for is friends, I can't ask for more;

I'm lying on my bed, my bed of straw
These people are evil, I'm lying on the floor.

Priyanka Patel & Georgia Grant-Anderson (11)
Furzedown Primary School

When Dino Died

To me he was the best dog in the world.
He was loving and gentle.

When he died a huge cloud cast a shadow over me.
He was gone and I was alone.
That's what happened when Dino died.

I remember him as just a small puppy.
I played with him.
He cheered me up.

When he died a huge cloud cast a shadow over me.
He was gone and I was alone.
That's what happened when Dino died.

I keep photos of him and I look at them.
I remember the good times we had.

When he died a huge cloud cast a shadow over me.
He was gone and I was alone.
That's what happened when Dino died.

Daniel Gollop (10)
Furzedown Primary School

Evacuee

Evacuee, yes, that's me,
Cold, sad and lonely.
I'm on the farm,
With the eggs in my arms,
Silently hoping I come to no harm.

Sad, confused, yes, that's me,
The sad confused evacuee.
I go to the field to pick some flowers,
The day's going to last for hours and hours.

Frightened, anxious, yes, that's me,
The frightened, anxious evacuee.
On the table I see
A letter from Mum addressed to me.

I read the letter,
And just stare.
It's there in black and white, look, she cares!

Happy and joyful, yes, that's me,
The happy and joyful evacuee.
I run to the field and play,
I know I'll be happy for the rest of the day!

Jessica Ramsay (11)
Furzedown Primary School

Until My Gran Died

When my hamster died I thought he was hibernating
But he did not look the same as normal,
I felt sad inside
That was until Gran died.
I thought I could handle dying,
That was until Gran died.

When my cat died she had lived for a long time
And then she passed away,
I felt hurt inside
That was until Gran died.
I thought I could handle dying,
That was until Gran died.

When my dog died she wasn't very old
And she got run over,
I felt gloomy inside
That was until Gran died.
I thought I could handle dying,
That was until Gran died.

When my gran died, tears poured down my face,
I knew it was the end of mine and Gran's relationship.
I thought I could handle dying,
That was until Gran died.

I think of my gran some days,
And deep inside, my heart has a real ache.

I miss my gran!

Stephanie Carruthers (10)
Furzedown Primary School

But Why Did Gran Die

I was very close to my gran
I lived with her
She smothered me with love.

I loved my gran
But why did she have to die?

My mum would come and visit me a lot
She loved my gran too.

I loved my gran
But why did she have to die?

A few years earlier
I remembered she wasn't well
I cried and cried.

I loved my gran
But why did she have to die?

She went into hospital and then came home.

I loved my gran
But why did she have to die?

She died in bed
We all went to her funeral
She got buried
And became one with the earth.

I loved my gran
But why did she have to die?

Joel Cameron Best (10)
Furzedown Primary School

Until Uncle Died

I lost my fish.
He got put down the toilet.
I didn't cry,
But I felt sad inside.

I thought
I could deal with funerals.
That was
Until Uncle died.

I had a cat.
He was really old.
He died of old age.
I buried him.
I didn't cry
But I felt sad inside.

I thought
I could deal with funerals.
That was
Until Uncle died.

I went to my uncle's funeral.
I saw people there,
Dressed in black.
How I cried, yes, I cried.

I thought
I could deal with funerals.
That was
Until Uncle died.

I miss my uncle now,
As I remember all the good times we shared
And the jokes he made.

Chelsee Ryan (11)
Furzedown Primary School

Graffiti

Drawing bad things on the wall
Who does it?
I do - when everyone is asleep in bed!
Why do I do it?
I love it!

What do I draw?
Sword through a heart
Someone smoking
Guns and bullets
Someone with a penknife in their head

Who hates it?
Old ladies tutting and pointing
Pushing their trolleys with their hunched backs
Hitting it with their bags and sticks
But I love graffiti
Even swear words on the toilet wall of McDonald's

And I like to draw in the dark
But no one sees me
Drawing bad things on the wall.

Jamayne Cassar (11) & Jannell Wilkie
Glenbrook Primary School

My Pet Poem

My pet is hot
My pet is cold
He does good tricks
Young and old

He slips and slides
Up and down
He plays all day
Until he falls to the ground.

Donte Knight
Glenbrook Primary School

The Streets

Around the streets there is a lot of violence.
Stop the violence, bring education.
Stop the crimes and murders.
There are too many people being killed.
Stop, please stop knives and guns.
We want a joyful world, not a devastated world.
Make peace and love, not blood.
Gangs are having fights with other gangs.
Police are being involved, having to take people to prison.
Like in the newspaper, a girl was taken away,
Her name was Madeleine.
Stop the robbing!
You could be walking round the corner and get shot or stabbed,
Stop please.
I am warning you, beware,
On the streets, anything could happen.

Jordayne Daley (7)
Glenbrook Primary School

All About My Grandma With Me

Hey, Grandma.
How you doing?
I hope you are peaceful alone.
All the days when you went to hospital.
I always cry because you brought joy to me.
I wish you were still with me, I love you.
I love you so much I wish you could hear every word I say.
Bye-bye Grandma, I love you so much.
When I hear your voice it reminds me of the bells' ring.
When you were with me you did not need to give me all the things
you did.
Whenever you need me, just shout out my name. 'Zaki!'

Zakiatu Seisay (7)
Glenbrook Primary School

My Magic Box

(Based on 'Magic Box' by Kit Wright)

I will put in my box . . .
A bunch of mad barking dogs,
A pinch of my second cousin's first words,
A grab of my grandparents' huge house.

I will put in my box . . .
A jugful of my brilliant birthday diamond,
A handful of magnificent memories of teachers,
A spoonful of my fantastic family all together.

I will put in my box . . .
A splash of my friends with me,
A pinch of memories of people I knew,
A spoonful of things I thought were beautiful.

My box is designed with a sun and a moon,
With gold stars and a diamond lock.
It slowly opens like a door into a valley.

I shall swim as fast as I can in my box on the bottom of a French sea,
Then I will be washed ashore onto a burning hot English beach,
The colour of a shimmering gold star next to the sun.

Matilda Handley (9)
Glenbrook Primary School

My Mother's Day Poem

Mothers are the best
Because they are always there for you
When you need them and when you don't.

They're very good
Because they can help you with your homework
And they cook and feed you.

Jade Curran (8)
Glenbrook Primary School

My Sister

Courteney's her name
She's like a cat but tame
She's as sweet as sugar
She runs around not making a sound
She's always playing a game
But she's our Courteney you see
I love her, she loves me
I'm there for her
She's there for me . . . she's like a shining star
Above the moon
When I'm crying she comes to say,
'Come on, Emma, don't cry.'
I start laughing and that's . . .
Why I love my sister.

Emma-Lisa Monahan (9)
Glenbrook Primary School

The Sunshine

The sun makes me warm.
The sun makes me relax.
It is so bright.
It makes me think of my country.
The sun reminds me of the desert.
It keeps everyone hot.
It gives light to the world.
I feel like nobody is around when I feel the sun.
I think the sun is wonderful.
Warmth is a good thing about the sun.
That it helps plants to grow.
So not dark is our world.
The sun, I will always be your friend.

Olaoluwa Olanrele (8)
Glenbrook Primary School

My Magical Box

(Based on 'Magic Box' by Kit Wright)

I will put in the box . . .
A handful of my nan's hugs,
A dash of Auntie's spicy food,
A jug of my brother's smile.

I will put in the box . . .
A dusting of my mum's love,
A sprinkle of my uncle's laugh,
A bag full of my first walk.

I will put in the box . . .
A spoonful of a shooting comet,
A bottle of my cousin's scream,
A splash of my sister's smiles.

My box is made of stained glass and dewdrops,
With diamonds and sapphires,
Its corners are made of sparkling crystals.

I shall glide on the rainbow,
Then slide down the other end, the colour of tigers' stripes.

Chantae Williams (9)
Glenbrook Primary School

My Little Baby Cousin

My little baby cousin
Is as cute as a teddy bear
She is so cuddly, warm and soft
She's like a smiling sun
I feel very passionate about my cousin
I feel full of joy like love birds together
And that's my little baby cousin.

Breanna Baker (10)
Glenbrook Primary School

Nail Polishes

The *colourful* nail polishes
I have lots at home
Shining, glimmering and rich-looking
Like a nail polish land polishing the land
As great as a rainbow
They make me feel I'm special
As if I'm an angel
The *colourful* nail polishes
They make me a star.

I can't explain why I like them
But they smell perfect
My mum is a professional.

The *colourful* nail polishes
All towered alone
Lonely, shimmering, silver
They can't rub off
Shining as a sun on my fingernails
Good as gold
I feel like a rock star
Like I'm famous
The *colourful* polishes
Remind me of being popular.

People are famous . . . it's because of *nail polishes!*

Laura Kieu Anh Le (10)
Glenbrook Primary School

My World

You are my sweetheart and my soul,
I love you so much that I want to explode.
You are my world and my pot of gold,
I'll still love you when you're old,
Because you are my soulmate and my world.
My love meets your love from the heavens
From up above and everyone needs love
In this big, beautiful world.
When the birds sing, it's Mum calling her baby chick
With its soft silky wings.
When baby chicks cry, there's always somewhere
That a bird is learning how to fly.

My world, my precious thing,
My mum is everything.

Kaleigh Balanta-Avalos (8)
Glenbrook Primary School

My Poem About Love

Love is beautiful.
Love is me.
If someone loves me
That will be sweet.
Red as roses
My cheeks can be.
As I said, love is me.
Be aware of love every day until the night comes.
Hearts and poems everywhere until the night of love.
Love is everywhere, love is in my heart.
It spins around like a dancing lady in the night of love.

Chynah Nicholls-Planter (9)
Glenbrook Primary School

Charlotte

Charlotte is as pretty as the Queen,
She has blonde and brown hair,
Kind, happy, sweet,
Like a cute fluffy puppy,
Like the warm sun on my face,
She makes me happy,
She makes my brother happy,
When she walks into the room,
She sparkles like the Queen,
Charlotte takes me to the park,
Everyone notices her,
She brightens up the place,
She is as sweet as a cherry,
Charlotte,
She is like an angel up in Heaven.

Alexandra Jones (9)
Glenbrook Primary School

My Nanny And Me

My nanny is the best
I think she is better than the rest.
My nanny went to Heaven when I was three
I hope she still remembers me.
I miss my nanny cuddling me
I miss her bouncing me on her knee.
I love my nanny and my nanny loves me.

My nanny is now an angel in the sky
I wish I could see her fly by.
I'd give her a great big hug and a kiss
And tell her how much she is missed.

Because I love my nanny and my nanny loves me.

Leah O'Connell (9)
Glenbrook Primary School

My Magic Box
(Based on 'Magic Box' by Kit Wright)

I will put in my box . . .
A splash of shining love from my family
A pinch of my best teacher and my class
A piece of the great world.

I will put in my box . . .
A handful of my gorgeous grandma
A pan of the loveliest days in Paris and Madrid.

I will put in my box . . .
A grab of love from my mum, dad and brother
A tablespoon of the best country in the world - England
A dash of my baby cousin's first words.

My box is designed with gold and silver glitter on the top
And fur for the handles
It slowly opens and closes making a squeaking noise.

I shall climb a mountain, the great Mount Everest
Then I shall swim in the River Thames
Beneath the colours of the sky and the sun.

Billy Bradan Hudson (9)
Glenbrook Primary School

My Special Sentimental Box
(Based on 'Magic Box' by Kit Wright)

I will put in my box . . .
A spoonful of my giggly baby cousin's laughter.
A dash of the bright yellow sun.
A sprinkle of rain to jump in the puddles.

My box is designed with photos of my friends and family,
With my memories in 2001.
It slowly opens with my favourite colour, pink.
I shall put the most comfortable chair in my box
So it's my own comfortable home.

Leighanne Gabrielle Brown (9)
Glenbrook Primary School

The Magic Box
(Based on 'Magic Box' by Kit Wright)

I will put in my box . . .
A pinch of my dad's perfume.
A handful of my dad's love.

I will put in my box . . .
A bowl full of my mum's love.
A spoonful of my mum's smell.

I will put in my box . . .
The love from me to my sister.

My box is decorated with diamonds
With shells and stars around the edge.
It's automatic and made out of glass.

I shall go to the best ice skating rink
On the coast of Ghana,
Then be washed ashore by the colourful sea.

Lamrana Jalloh (9)
Glenbrook Primary School

My Magic Box
(Based on 'Magic Box' by Kit Wright)

In my magic box I will put . . .
A bed made out of cotton to sleep in
A river of melted chocolate
And a blue jacuzzi for some time off

I will have a plasma TV with cherry-coloured diamonds on it
A crystal fish bowl with vanilla-coloured fish in it
And I will have a sunset, orange-coloured for my iPod.

In my magic box I will have . . .
Two olive-green roses with rubies in the centre
Some blue water from the Atlantic Ocean
And a lock of Goldilocks' hair.

Michael Allen (9)
Glenbrook Primary School

I Will Put In My Box

(Based on 'Magic Box' by Kit Wright)

I will put in my box . . .
A splash of my daddy's hugs.
A handful of my mum's kisses.
A bottle full of my auntie's cuddles.

I will put in my box . . .
A sprinkle of my sister's smile.
A bag full of my nanna's dinner.
A jug full of my favourite colour.

I will put in my box . . .
A pouch full of my good grandma's favourite food.
A cupful of my baby brother's brilliant football goals
A bath full of my wonderful uncle's brilliant jokes.

My box is made out of ice-cold crystals and angel wings
With a lid of gold rainbows and silver sprinkles.
Its lock is made from a golden jewel.

I shall wave with the dolphins' fins
Then dive into an ocean the colour of rose petals.

Dontai Stewart (8)
Glenbrook Primary School

I Will Put In The Box . . .

(Based on 'Magic Box' by Kit Wright)

I will put in the box . . .
A sprinkle of my mum's smiles.
A dash of my nephew's laughs.

I will put in the box . . .
A spoonful of my brother's voice.
A scrape of my auntie's cookies.

I will put in the box . . .
A scoop of my favourite sights.
A bottle of my mum's favourite water place.

Christian Ogiugo (9)
Glenbrook Primary School

The Magic Box

(Based on 'Magic Box' by Kit Wright)

I will put in the box . . .
A pinch of my mum's lovely love.
A sprinkle of my brother's kisses.
A spoon of my baby sister's kicks.

I will put in the box . . .
A dusting of my tastiest pizza.
A handful of my honey ice cream.
A dollop of my milkshake.

My box is made of red rose petals
With a rainbow and dewdrops.

I shall dance with my family in the sky with the moon
Then I will go to sleep.

Daniella Parreira (8)
Glenbrook Primary School

The Magic Box

(Based on 'Magic Box' by Kit Wright)

I will put in my box . . .
A dish of my lovely love.
A trickle of my family's poetic pride.
A slice of my dad's delicious recipes.

I will put in my box . . .
A scrape of my favourite fabulous country.
A glass of my first tingly touch.

My box is made from red rubies and rainbows
With a lid of decorated flower roots.
Its key is made from a hook.

I shall fly in my box as the rainbows come to life
On the biggest hills of rainbows.
Then slide down the colourful rainbow.

Sundis Hassan (9)
Glenbrook Primary School

My Fabulous Fantastic Box

I will put in the box . . .
A drop of my spectacular sister's hugs,
A pinch of my mum's kisses,
A scoop of my special grandad's smiles.

I will put in the box . . .
A slice of my friend's giggles,
A splash of my mum's love,
A jar of my dad's cuddles.

My box is made of crystals and gold,
With a lid of rainbow and green emeralds,
Its lock is made of a lion's tooth.

I shall ride on a dinosaur's back on the grass in the jungle,
Then have a race with another dinosaur,
                              the colour of green emeralds.

Henry Elezi (8)
Glenbrook Primary School

I Will Put In The Box

(Based on 'Magic Box' by Kit Wright)

I will put in the box . . .
A bash of my auntie's hugs,
A bowl of my grandad's joy,
A dollop of my brother's gurgles.

I will put in the box . . .
A sprinkle of the colour of my eyes,
And the smell of my parents,
And a spoonful of the soft snow.

My box is made of spicy thorns with stars on the top.
Its lock is made of a python's tooth.

I shall climb a candyfloss mountain in my box
And splash into the mountain which is the colour of the brain.

Jamal Brown (8)
Glenbrook Primary School

My Magic Box

(Based on 'Magic Box' by Kit Wright)

I will put in my box . . .
My mum's kisses,
My sister's giggles,
A diamond from ancient times.

I will put in my box . . .
The dolphins in the ocean,
A picture from my sister,
My mum and sister's love.

I will put in my box . . .
Crystals from Roman times,
The last gold on Earth,
The oldest portrait.

I will put in my box . . .
My first birthday,
My mum's hugs,
My sister's kisses.

I will put in my box . . .
Thirty-three golden wishes,
A bucket of love,
A jug of hugs.

My box is surrounded by stars
And the lock is made of iron.
I will glide in my box across the rainbow
Like a bird.

Jay Payne (9)
Glenbrook Primary School

I Will Put In The Box
(Based on 'Magic Box' by Kit Wright

I will put in the box . . .
A handful of my baby brother's kisses,
A jug of my family's love,
A drop of my favourite sights.

I will put in the box . . .
A scoop of my mum's favourite dishes,
A pinch of my special mum's smile,
A slice of my big brother's funny jokes.

I will put in the box . . .
A dollop of my favourite recipe,
A dusting of my friend's friendship,
A trickle of my family's hugs.

I will put in the box . . .
A bottle of my favourite times,
A bag full of my baby's first smile,
A splash of my friend's love.

My box is made of diamond petals
With a lid of tiger skin.
Its locks are made of tigers' nails.

I shall sail in my box on the top of the clouds
In a beautiful shining sky,
The colour of a shining crystal-green emerald.

Christabel Darlington (9)
Glenbrook Primary School

My Magic Box

(Based on 'Magic Box' by Kit Wright)

I will put in the box . . .
A handful of my parents' love,
A scoop of a giggle with my friends,
A splash of my cousin's company.

I will put in the box . . .
A jug of my first day at school,
A dust of roses' smell,
A drop of the shooting stars.

I will put in the box . . .
A mouthful of my friendship,
A bottle of my mum's recipes,
A jar of Miss Higginson's teaching.

My box is made of snakeskin and dewdrops
With a lid of glowing crystals.
Its lock is made of dazzling shiny diamonds.

I shall climb a colourful rainbow in the bright blue sky
Then slide down and hang from a rainbow,
The colour of a twinkle in my mum's eyes.

Tania Freitas (8)
Glenbrook Primary School

My Attractive And Pleasing Box

(Based on 'Magic Box' by Kit Wright)

I will put in my box . . .
A cup of my sister's first birthday,
A pound of my dad's sizzling and tickling moustache
On my fragile cheek,
And a handful of my mum's marvellous, sweet, loving care
And kindness.

I will put in my box . . .
A pinch of my teacher's sweet smell and care,
A sprinkle of my family's and grandma's good nourishment,
And a glance of my delicious, designed dumplings.

Elizabeth Shokan (9)
Glenbrook Primary School

The Magic Box
(Based on 'Magic Box' by Kit Wright)

I will put in the box . . .
A pinch of my mum's cuddly kisses,
A dusting of my dad's lovely laughs,
A scoop of my auntie's special love.

I will put in the box . . .
A splash of my favourite colour pink,
A fresh smell of my favourite flowers,
A dusting of my favourite chicken paté.

My box is made of shiny pebbles,
With a lid made of diamonds,
Its lock is made of red rubies.

I shall swim with dolphins in my box, on the sea ocean,
Then surf on the sea ocean, the colour of diamonds.

Kashira Green (8)
Glenbrook Primary School

The Magic Box
(Based on 'Magic Box' by Kit Wright

I will put in the box . . .
A jar of my mum's cute kisses
A scoop of my soft cat's miaows
A drop of my baby brother's funny laughter.

I will put in the box . . .
A spoonful of my cat's big cuddles
A bottle of my dog's crying
A bag full of the smell of a lovely rose

I will put in the box . . .
A carton of bright yellow flowers
A handful of blue bright sky
A scrap of my mum's huge bear hugs.

Liam Dixon (8)
Glenbrook Primary School

I Will Put In My Box

(Based on 'Magic Box' by Kit Wright)

I will put in the box . . .
A pinch of my mum's kiss,
A spoonful of my dad's love,
A dash of my mum's kiss
And my dad's huge hug.

I will put in the box . . .
A dash of my dad's smartness
And my mum's smile
And a pinch of me
And my mum's beauty.

Mickel Cerio (9)
Glenbrook Primary School

All About Football

Football
It is an amazing sport
There are so many legends
Magnificent, glorious and joyful
Like a bright golden sunset
Like the shimmering warm sea
I feel like it is my life's dream to play football
Football . . .
It makes me glow as bright as the sun
And makes me feel happy and safe.

Ibrahim Diallo (9)
Glenbrook Primary School

The Future Is Near

The future is very near
Come and I will tell you what is near.
You never know before you hear,
Cars will be flying in the air.
With trains in the air
Or aeroplanes flying in the sky.
Radios that are touch-screen
And fancy computers.

What if you could go into the future and explore time.
What if you could go into the computer world
And see what your friends are e-mailing you online.
What if you could go to the underworld.
What if you could go into the sky.
What if you could go up into Heaven.
What if you could swoop down to London.

Shawn Boothe-Ewerse (9)
Shaftesbury Park Primary School

My Head

My head feels like an imaginary thing.
It is an alarm that goes ding-a-ling-a-ling.
It controls my body, I don't know why
But I wish it could make the whole world fly.

When you are in a deep, deep world,
Your head feels like it twirls and twirls.
You don't realise you're being controlled
By some little brother's different modes.

My head has made me write this all
But my work might by withdrawn.

Edward Vemba (11)
Shaftesbury Park Primary School

Making The Day Happy

Let the sun shine every day.
You don't really have to pay.
You can go and sit and watch the bay.
You can go to the fête and have a good day.

You can have a lie in and have a good day.
You can play with clay every day.
You may have a good day.
You might have a rainy day.

Let the day shine every day.
You may have a happy day.
You might have a lucky day.

Nicole Warwick Weeks (10)
Shaftesbury Park Primary School

Making The World A Better Place

Making the world a better place
So people don't worry about colour and race.

Making the world a happy and a lovely place,
Making the world happy and the people smile every day.
Making the world a place where people are happy.

But, however, we can work together to make the world a better place
Or pray to God and tell Him to make us happy
And also make the world a better place.

For some people who care about each other,
They have big hearts to care for us.
Think of people who are poor or people who don't have any money.
So let's help the people who are poor
And make the world a better place for them.

Kimberley Valdez (9)
Shaftesbury Park Primary School

To Make A Better Place

We all know we can't change the world.
But, we can make it a better place.
Some people say they know what to do.
Then why don't we do something about it?
Things are sometimes good and sometimes bad.
Let's work to make things better.
So put your hands together and pray.
Think of the lives we can save today.
What can *you* accomplish to help
The people that are fighting alone?
If we all do our bit today,
We can make a better place for the children of today.

Kamisha Acheampong (9)
Shaftesbury Park Primary School

The World

The world is a place with guns and knives.
The world is a place that is scary at night.
There are some parts of the world that I don't like.
The world is a place that gives me a fright.

The world is a place that could be changed.
The world is sometimes a beautiful sight.
The world is a word with five letters.
The world is a place that, in my imagination, is better.

The world is a place with different races.
Made up of people with different faces.
And, if my imagination does come true,
The world will be a better place for me and for you.

King Stewart-Taylor (8)
Shaftesbury Park Primary School

Friendship, Fun And Friends

Friendship

Friends are for friendship,
Friends are for fun,
Friends are for everyone,
Friends are always together
And going to be forever.

Fun

Friends always have fun,
Fun is always for friends,
Friends are like flowers
They live in beautiful towers
Just like feathers.

Friends

Ships can be sailing on the sea,
And friends can still be together happily.
Friends have blissful times
And down in the dumps times.

But they will always be together
Each and every time.
Try and find your friends in your heart
That is where I found mine.

Kirsty Welch & Leanne Powell (10)
Shaftesbury Park Primary School

The Future

Look! Today people are dying.
Souls have been taken, families crying.

What about the future, will it change?

Imagining the world is a better place
Poor people and rich come face to face.

What about the future, will it change?

Children get bullied and often cry.
They go home and feel like they want to die.

What about the future, will it change?

People want to have a better life.
Not with the present trouble and strife.

What about the future, will it change?

Think about the next generation.
They should not face fear and frustration.

What about the future, will it change?

Children have nightmares and wake up with fright,
Wondering what their future will be like.

I would like people's lives to be rearranged
And let's hope, the *future* will be changed.

Longelini Vemba (9)
Shaftesbury Park Primary School

Fear

Fear is hot colours of red, orange and yellow.
Never show fear to a dog or your fellow.
Fear is hot like lava,
Fear is dark like a cave.
Sometimes you feel like you're lost in a maze.

Boy when you're scared, time doesn't fly,
Look at Big Ben, it will help you with the time.
Big Ben is your friend,
Boy, now time flies.

Fear scares people,
It scares people like me and you,
Look in the sky it will go away,
That's what I do.

Fear sometimes brings tears,
But be strong like The Three Musketeers,
Then there is no need to feel sad,
Also no need to go mad.

Jacob Taylor (10)
Shaftesbury Park Primary School

Pet Cats

Cute and furry,
Make a good pet,
This little animal doesn't like to get wet.

Pounces at night,
Miaows at its prey,
It's happy to jump and run around all day.

Springs into the air, needs lots of care,
Loves to explore and see the world, just a little bit more.
Love their food and put me in a good mood.

That's why I love pet cats.

Elizabeth Turner (10)
Shaftesbury Park Primary School

Happiness

If you're sad,
Look into the blue sky
With Heaven up there,
And God a very pleasant guy,
And the white clouds relax in the sky.

I'm always happy, never sad,
Oh yes, never really mad.
I like adventures, mysteries too
And also exploring, do you too?

Football, tennis and swimming are my hobbies,
They are really enjoyable.
I am smart and I really like to think
I have a great imagination
Like humans living in sinks.

Kiye Martin (10)
Shaftesbury Park Primary School

Wandering In The Sky

Every now and then I wander in the blue sky.
I look at the blazing sun.
I say to myself, 'Do the birds and other things
In the sky ever fall right through the clouds?'
I love the sky.

But sometimes I don't like the sky
Because all I see is lightning bolts.
Danger!
Which strikes fear into my heart.

But sometimes the sky is glorious
With its pink and orange sight.
I gaze at I all evening,
I remember how I feel inside.

Roshauna Hinds-Blackwood (10)
Shaftesbury Park Primary School

Dreams

When I am bored I dream
About things I haven't seen.
Elephants that fly, houses on clouds,
Barking pigs and miaowing cows.
We lived on Mars
And there were legs on cars!

When I am bored I dream
About things I have seen.
If teachers gave us our way
We would dance and cheer all day.
When we go home the party begins,
In the pool dolphins flap their fins.

When I am bored I dream
About things that I want,
Like jewellery fit for a queen.
I'd love to win Little Laureates,
Not being mean, just very keen.

Francoise Savizon (10)
Shaftesbury Park Primary School

Friendship

Friendship is just so sweet,
Me and my friend you can never beat.
When you're lonely talk to a friend
You will never want your friendship to end.

Always help each other
Don't go mad at one another.
Sometimes you have your ups and downs
When you shout at each other, it's not a great sound.

Friendship, friendship!
Let me give you a tip,
Never split up with your close friends
Always stick together till the end!

Emily Hignell (11)
Shaftesbury Park Primary School

Box

The shape of a cube,
Colour of the sea.
What's inside
A man, woman or a horse running free?

I'll give you a clue,
Every now and again.
I'll dish out a few
To help you out my friend.

A gold locket,
Earrings too.
A whole catwalk,
Maybe one or two.

Here's a clue,
It's what I want to be.
A vet, a nurse,
Or have a chocolate factory?

OK, do you give up?
I'll tell you.
My hopes and dreams
And others too.

Mariah Laurent (11)
Shaftesbury Park Primary School

In The Future

I've got extraordinary neighbours
With lightsabers.
I've got a flying car,
That can go so far.
When I open my door,
There's a robot mopping my floor.
I've got the latest PlayStation,
It is know for its precision.

Reiss Hanks Headley (10)
Shaftesbury Park Primary School

Beauty In The Sky

As I look outside
I see the sun rise.
On a beautiful fine day
I see people dancing
While I am glancing
And they shout, 'Hip hip hooray!'

As I look outside
And I see the moon shine
As it never shone before.
It is a beautiful sight
As it glows in the night
Just want to see more and more.

As I look outside
And I say goodnight to the sky.
As I go to bed
The stars fade away
And they say, 'See you another day.'
And I say, 'Bye-bye!'

Tadiwa Albert (11)
Shaftesbury Park Primary School

What Happened On The Football Pitch

I like football, it's the best,
The football pitch is muddy,
Players are dirty and slimy,
Some boots are orange, then at the end
They are black and muddy.

The keeper is clean and then he gets the slime.
The fans say, 'Who are ya!'
The players' drinks are nice and cold.
After the game the players are clean
When they wash off the slimy mud.
When I'm playing my feet get stuck in the mud!

Jack Cottier (10)
Shaftesbury Park Primary School

My Dream Is . . .

My dream is to be a footballer
A striker, that's my position.
When I score a goal I jump up in the air
Winning the cup would be an accomplishment.

My dream is to become a swimmer
To swim in the deep end so I can join my friends.
I love to swim, it's great.
It makes me fit, especially healthy.

Oh my god!
I've seen my dreams
And I've heard about these things.
Maybe I'll try these things out
Now if you want me to, give me a shout.

Amy Bergin (9)
Shaftesbury Park Primary School

Football

People play with their hearts and souls,
People play in different roles.
Some people get really hurt,
Some people fall down in the dirt.

Some people have brilliant skills,
Footballers eat healthy meals.
Some people are really fast,
One football team must finish last.

Football pitches are in good condition,
Football scouts are on a mission
To go and find a young addition.
That could be anyone.

That's why I love football.

Danny Davies (11)
Shaftesbury Park Primary School

Imagine A School

Imagine a school without:

Teachers telling us what to do,
Children thinking children rule.
Everyone has good style,
Me and my mates are head of the school.

Imagine a school without:

Bullying,
A school that's cursed,
Uniform!
Really nice teachers understand the worst.

Imagine a school with:

No rules,
Jewellery allowed,
You can wear your own clothes
And speak out proud!

Imagine a school with:

A chocolate fountain,
A chocolate swimming pool . . .
Oh, did I mention
Chocolate rules!

Imagine a school with:

Roller coasters in the playground
And every day you get a hundred pounds.
You get your own phone
And people don't moan!

Oh don't you wish all that was real.

Lauren Hines-Clarke (10)
Shaftesbury Park Primary School

Love

Love is in the heart,
Love is in the mind.

But when it comes to Valentine's,
Love spreads all around.
Hugs, kisses, cards and presents too.
This is how we share the love from me to you.

Love is in the heart,
Love is in the mind.

What would it feel like without love?
When you see two lovely doves
You feel like no one loves you anymore
But you can find your true love but . . .
Who?

Love is in the heart,
Love is in the mind.

There's loads of love,
There's family love,
There's friends' love,
And there's love.

Love is in the heart,
Love is in the mind.

I love all my friends.
I love all my family.
They're the things that matter in life . . .
Love!

Love is in the heart,
Love is in the mind.

This is the end of my poem
So remember what I said.

Love is in the heart,
Love is in the mind.

Chloe Morris   (10)
Shaftesbury Park Primary School

I Enjoy School

I enjoy Shaftesbury Park School
But I wish it had a pool.
My best subject is PE
And my other one is ICT,

The best thing about this school is
The people don't act like fools.
My teacher is a funny one
And I bet he eats a hot cross bun.

I like the people in this school,
All the people rock and rule.
Even if they are not cool.
So this is a great school.

Jack Mulligan (9)
Shaftesbury Park Primary School

I Wish . . .

I wish the world were a safer place,
I wish people wouldn't judge other people's race.
I wish every child could go to school,
I wish everybody was absolutely cool.

I wish people were enormously happy,
I wish babies would grow out of nappies.
I wish I had cool PS2 games,
I wish people wouldn't call other people names.

I wish clowns weren't scary,
I wish werewolves weren't hairy.
I wish radios weren't loud,
I wish there weren't grey clouds.

Adnan Amidu (9)
Shaftesbury Park Primary School

Future

New gadgets, new games,
New trainers, new names,
Hover boots, flying cars,
Green ugly Martians from Mars.
Smells of metal in the air,
Helpful robots everywhere.
Xbox 5,000, PlayStation 20,
If you need a robot there are plenty.
Silver houses, silver doors, silver ceilings, silver floors,
New planets, new cities, new countries.
New shops, new subjects in school,
Like maths plus one and science in a pool.
I wish the future was now, it sounds so cool.

Joe Sadler (10)
Shaftesbury Park Primary School

Secret Box

Under my bed I keep seven boxes with seven locks.
All the things I need to hide are safe inside.

My rings, my tins, my fish,
My magic book of spells!
I could turn a fish into a bird just in a whoosh!
And I could change December into summer.

I could clap my hands and stare at a balloon
And watch the moon come floating to my window sill
And one day I will . . .

Abdikarim Abdi (9)
Shaftesbury Park Primary School

It Has . . .

Sharp teeth
It's a hunter
Big fins
Devil eyes
A furious fighter
Fast swimmer
It's powerful
Scary claws
Licks people's faces,
Jumps high,
Growls at people.

What am I?
Can you guess?
I am bigger than the rest.

Ashley Sylvester (10)
Shaftesbury Park Primary School

Sport

Sport is very healthy
It will make you wealthy.
Never take the chance to let it go,
If you asked me to play it, I wouldn't say no!

There are many sports like tennis and rugby,
Although my best one is football.
You can score many goals in football.
The best position is striker.

My favourite skill that I like
Is the step over
A football needs to be hard
Or you can't play real football.

Alley Hamadouch (9)
Shaftesbury Park Primary School

I Had A Dream

I had a dream to be a fashion designer,
My mum wants to be a super child minder.

I had a dream to be a fantastic vet,
So I could look after people's beautiful pets.

I had a dream to be in a family pub,
I'd love to be in a family club.

It is your chance!

Chloe Welch (10)
Shaftesbury Park Primary School

About My Mum

I know that sometimes I get on your nerves.
You look in the mirror, I see your curves.

You smile like you've won the lottery
I think you should do pottery!

You make everyone happy
Except when you are snappy.

Roses are red, violets are blue,
Everyone will love you and that will do!

Charlie John Morris (10)
Shaftesbury Park Primary School

A Shining Star

As it shines and glows in the dark, maybe for you
And then your heart is filled with a dramatic happiness
For when you're down and blue
You'll wake up with the rising sun and you will say
My star is waiting for me, she's waiting behind
And for the golden sun to end its day tonight.
I stare and look cos I know she's waiting for me.

Autumn Reid (9)
Shaftesbury Park Primary School

I Have A Dream

I have a dream to be a footballer,
I have a dream to reach that goal.

I have a dream to be like Henry,
To me he is my favourite celebrity.

I have a dream to be a tennis player,
To move my feet like a cheetah.

I have a dream to be a number one player,
To slam the ball like thunder.

I have a dream to be a basketball player,
To dribble and shoot around the key.

I have a dream to be a forward,
To beat the defenders and in the net.

Che Gibbens (10)
Shaftesbury Park Primary School

I Am The Person Who . . .

I am the person who gets kicked and punched,
I am the person who has no money for lunch.
I am the person who is always crushed,
I am the person who . . .
I am the person who sits alone,
I am the person who gets a phone and no return.
I am the person who thought it would never end,
I am the person who . . .
I am the person who no one sticks up for,
I am the person who gets laughed at
Whispered:
I am the person who . . .

Ky-Ann Dumetz (10)
Shaftesbury Park Primary School

A Cat

A furry pet
So cute and fun.

A pet you can have,
It is as mad as you think.

They love lots of tuna,
And they sleep a lot.

You can sit down and . . .
They follow you lots.

Go out the door,
It will look out of the window.

You should get new toys,
Or it will not play.

Imogen Connolly-Leach (9)
Shaftesbury Park Primary School

Dogs

They bark like they talk,
They love to go for walks.
They jump all around,
They dribble on the ground.

They love to drink and eat,
They enjoy their long sleep.
They leap when they want a treat,
They can dig a hole very deep.

They love their owners if they treat them nice,
They cannot put on them a price.
They are bought at a fantastic cost,
They can find their way home if they are lost.

Francis Barry (9)
Shaftesbury Park Primary School

Christmas

The cheers of a child playing in the snow,
The sweet sound of their soft, delightful singing.
I like it on Christmas Day when you see everyone smiling,
Great big hugs and families getting presents.
The joy of all, especially the young.

I can see the crunchy white snowflakes beneath my feet
Separate and move from each other.
You tear frantically away the paper covered with patterns
Which doesn't matter when once torn.

I smell the turkey.
Such time and effort put into preparing it,
Let alone cooking the turkey
For everyone to enjoy.

I smell gunpowder, damp in the air,
Set off five minutes before
Letting off wonderful colours
And great big bangs.

Today's the day we celebrate Jesus' birth
When once greatness began
For extraordinary miracles that changed our world.

Generations, in years to come
We now know will change
But keep its spirit
But now we celebrate the presents.

Courtney Karl Foster (11)
Stanford Primary School

Happiness

Sounds like happy children playing outside,
Tastes like sweet berries, so tasty and nice,
Smells like pretty flowers in the summer and spring,
Looks like bright stars in the night sky,
It reminds me of my dearest friends.

Naheyan Gafoor (10)
Stanford Primary School

Rapid Summer

A s summer rapidly passes by
  we don't know what autumn has in store for the sky.
  people without their jumpers think that they're tough
  but really inside they're really rough.

U nforeseen, it feels like winter
  has mysteriously taken over the atmosphere
  which was tender.

T o torment us? Who knows
  people standing in rows
  waiting to buy the latest offers
  raiding the shops as if they're robbers.

U turns people make
  their cars clatter just like a rake.

M umbling and gossiping about people

N othing to talk about, just turn the roundabout
  there's a different road ahead.

Tysdayle Morrison (11)
Stanford Primary School

Roses

Roses are love, the red's perfect,
Sounds like flying birds in the breeze,
They look pretty and cute,
Taste like mouth-watering strawberry milkshakes,
Smell like lovely twinkling perfume,
Sparkling thorns on the stem,
Feel like soft bouncing beds.
The sweet colours of the roses,
The pink, red and the white
Make you smile
And also remind you of the first day of summer.

Nirali Khanderia (10)
Stanford Primary School

Jamaica

J is for Jamaica, the place where I was born.
A is for all my lovely memories from my relaxing home.
M is Marley, the Rastafarian, Bob Marley.
A is for amazing fun in the blazing sun.
I is for indulgence which equals happiness.
C is for coconuts, juicy, luscious coconuts.
A is for apples, lovely and sweet apples.

Mahalia Barnes (11)
Stanford Primary School

Hate

Hate is a gloomy, dark colour.
Hate sounds like the sizzle of a fire.
Hate tastes like poisonous venom.
Hate smells like a burn.
Hate looks evil like a devil.
Hate feels like a ghost inside you.
Hate gives a feedback of death.

Muazzam Begg (11)
Stanford Primary School

Friends

Friends are there in times of trouble,
Whether you have a double.

Friends are forever, they never let you down,
Your friendship is like a circle that goes round, round, round.

They say that friends should always stay together,
Whatever the weather, friends *forever!*

Mishaal Mehmood (11)
Stanford Primary School

Darkness

Darkness is pitch-black,
Someone is waiting to attack.
Darkness is the feeling of someone all alone,
Or a teenager without a mobile phone.
In a world of darkness it's very dreary,
With the face of someone scary,
So let's bring some lightness in,
And put darkness in the bin.

Angel Brown (11)
Stanford Primary School

Summer

S ummer is for fun and games
U nder the shady tree nice and cool
M ums and dads with their families in the hot sun
M aking sandcastles, having fun
E ating delicious strawberry lollies
R unning in the hot sun and playing games
            and wearing your nice summer clothes.

Payal Gosai (10)
Stanford Primary School

Summer

S urprising breeze
U tterly hot
M orning sleep
M elting ice cream
E ating lollies
R esting in the sand.

Aaron Wildman (11)
Stanford Primary School

The Colour

Dazzling, vivid, vibrant colour,
Bright, stinging my eyes like a shooting star.
How can a colour be made so bright
On everything you see at night?

Mixed with other colours makes it better,
Different shades add to the fun,
Cut out pictures and use as stencils
In any shape or size, no limits.

On books and paper, every page,
Clothes and chairs worn again,
Toys and games
Made exciting for all.

The colour is brilliant and so vividly true,
As bright as light through.
But what is the colour?
As you may have guessed, it's blue.

Samuel Cordner-Matthews (10)
Stanford Primary School

Barbados

B eautiful island in the sun
A place where friends and me have fun!
R ice and peas
B ananas too
A re good for me and you
D ogs and cats have their wars
O h, what for?
S o here I am at the beach
          where I can see the spectacular sea!

Tarna Elaine Jordan (10)
Stanford Primary School

Dear Hate

Why do you cause wars?
Break-ups of families and friends?
The list never ends.

But I guess we could stop it.
That all depends.

If only all the guns would vanish
Along with the bombs and poisonous gases.

Maybe then we could manage
To forget hate

And join together
In peace and harmony.

Seval Ahmet (11)
Stanford Primary School

Sticky Bubblegum

Mary had some bubblegum sticking to her hair,
She pulled and pulled at it until it went everywhere.
She tugged and heaved and got it out and she really didn't care.

She stuck it in her mouth,
She chewed and chewed at it and she knew her gum
was sure to blow!
The bubble got bigger and popped in someone's hair but she
knew it was going to go on Moe.

Mary got some bubblegum every single day,
She does the same thing all the time
But this time at school she didn't eat it,
She just drank lemon and lime.

Jade Cobham (8)
Stanford Primary School

Hunger, Poverty And Peace

Every day I see the way
A mother cries over hunger and depression.
Hunger grows, but peace does not.

Every day I see the way
Children get evacuated because of no peace.
They're homeless and they can't fend for themselves.
Homelessness grows, but peace does not.

Every day I see the way
People lie on the street, full of fear.
Poverty grows but peace does not.
But, what I want to know is,
When will there be peace?

Yinka Aina (10)
Stanford Primary School

Which School

I've come back from school to open a letter,
Which hopefully will decide someone's future.
Wilson's, Wallington, St Joseph's, which school shall it be?
Which school has chosen me?
I must open this letter or I might just die of tension
The decision is in the hands of God,
Please let the letter give me a nod.
I'm opening the letter,
I'm finding out what I have done,
If I pass then I will have great fun.
What does the letter say,
'I'm happy to tell you,' is what it says,
I think I know what the rest is, *hooray, hooray, hooray!*

Syed Imran Hyder (11)
Stanford Primary School

Million-Dollar Spy Poem

Spies and gadgets may be cool,
But remember, don't get caught or you will be called a fool.
You live in top-secret locations,
But you are still mysterious when you go on vacations.

You can have meetings underground,
And you can steal millions of pounds.
You disguise your identity so you're not recognised
But you're in prison before you realise.

People may become suspicious,
But you don't have to threaten them by being vicious.
Spies have to stay away from a life of crime,
If they don't have the patience to do the time.

When the police and FBI are on your case,
You have to be prepared to be chased.
You have to be a really good spy to know what it takes,
Because if you're not highly qualified you might make mistakes.

Spies drive in fast and customised cars,
And also get arrested in casino bars.
Spies are everywhere in an impossible disguise
And they can surprise you right before your eyes.

Earle Peterson (9)
Stanford Primary School

Winter

W ith all the snow that covers the floor
 I want lots of it, more, more, more
N ight and day it is still bitter
T he snow on the ground sparkles like glitter
E nd of the day, I've used up my time
R eady for tomorrow, it's mine, mine, mine.

Maisie Hartwell (10)
Stanford Primary School

May The 11th

Walking to school
Feeling the fear
SATs tests were here
Never thought I'd feel so scared.

Finally when I arrived
I went to the gym
And found a surprise.

All the tables were set
Metre by metre
And all of them were
Only one-seater.

When SATs were over
There was great relief.
A party was had and everyone was happy
That SATs had gone.

The only fear that was left
In everyone's mind
Were the results

Chandni Patel (11)
Stanford Primary School

Great Italy

I've gone to Rome,
Seen the Coliseum and St Peter's dome.

Went to Naples and Milan,
Ate at a restaurant, had a flan.

Half-past ten,
Heard an orchestra full of men.

Went to the beach
And ate a peach.

I've got to run,
But I've had lots of fun.

Alessia Mobile (11)
Stanford Primary School

The Boy In Hunger

The boy was in hunger
And the rain was getting stronger.

The boy's face was getting grey
And it was raining all the way.

He went down to the kitchen
But there was nothing to eat

Except there was a little treat
At Daddy's feet.

Abdul Hamid Naji (10)
Stanford Primary School

Love

Love is like a girl laughing,
Tastes like warm chocolate cookies.
When you see it, it looks like two people holding hands
                              having fun and laughing.
Smells like a beautiful perfume crawling up your shirt.
Happiness is sweet, love is beautiful,
Love is to keep.

Precious Oni (11)
Stanford Primary School

War

War is bad,
And makes soldiers' families very sad.
Bombs touch people with explosive stuff,
Just like blind man's bluff.
Peace, on the other hand, gives welfare,
But war abolishes care.
We should stop acting like barbarian fools,
And fix wars using friendship tools.

Shafee Latif (10)
Stanford Primary School

Magnificent

M arvellous glory
A fter the party
G lorious fun
N on-stop entertainment
I n or outside enjoyment
F un for all the family
I t's especially for the children
C ertainly stuff for adults
E nthusiastic games for all the family
N othing but fun and relaxation
T ell your friends and the fun will never end.

Kieran Alibaba (10)
Stanford Primary School

March 1st

I'm on my way to school.
As I pass the houses
I feel nervous.
Cars are passing,
Friends are calling,
People are speaking,
Babies are screaming.
I just wish I could stay at home all day.
What score am I going to get?
Am I going to pass or fail?
I don't know but I wish I did.

Thatiksha Thavathesan (10)
Stanford Primary School

Cyprus

The travel there took hours,
I even fell asleep,
In my head I was dreaming
And even counting sheep.

The plane had finally settled
And I was back on the ground
But better yet in Cyprus
And could barely make a sound.

The apartment there was lovely
And very cosy too
But what I really liked
Was there was lots of stuff to do.

We went onto the beach
With sand between our toes
There was a sea of people
As the saying goes.

When my holiday finally ended
I was very sad to go
But I had such a lot of fun
At all the late night shows.

Like I said the plane took hours
I even fell asleep
And in my head I was dreaming
But not of fluffy sheep.

Harleigh Swaine (10)
Stanford Primary School

Monday Mornings

Monday mornings give me a scare,
As I wake up from bed,
I toss and turn wishing I could turn the clocks back.
I eat with fright . . .
As the number calculations pop into my head.
As I walk out of the door I feel much happier.

I walk and walk,
I see cars racing up and down.
This reminds me of my teacher,
Always giving out sums.
I try to answer quick but time flies.
I'm at the school gate feeling tense.

I walk and walk towards the door,
And sit on a chair,
Ready to do a test.
I feel scared and don't know what happens next.
The test is over,
And I'm anxious for my score.
This wasn't any test . . .
It was a SATs test.

Nicole Ayettey (10)
Stanford Primary School

Arsenal

A mazing team
R uling the world
S ensational players
E mirates stadium
N ever-ending
A rsenal are the best
L ong lasting.

Dominic McEwen (9)
Stanford Primary School

The Last Day

I got out of bed,
I shout, 'Hooray!'
I'm ecstatic,
The last day.

I try to get ready,
As fast as I can,
My smile growing
As I ran.

I get to school
Just in time
I wait and wait
As minutes fly by.

Five more minutes
I'm watching the clock
Tension builds,
The doors should unlock.

As the teacher
Opens the door
I run for my life,
It's school no more.

Sharmin Gafoor (10)
Stanford Primary School

Anger

Anger is like lava blasting out of a red volcano.
Anger sounds like guns shooting through your mind.
Anger tastes like a spicy chilli burning in your mouth.
Anger smells like bacon burning under a grill.
Anger looks like trembling blood on delicate skin.
Anger feels like daggers in your back.
It reminds me of a lion scratching its furry skin.
It moves fiercely round me, unexpectedly waiting.

Ria Gudka (9)
Stanford Primary School

Why is School So Boring?

Why is school so boring?
I can't wake up in the morning,
While I am working, I am snoring,
I look so adoring,
I hate it when I am touring,
Even when my teacher is talking,
I open my tray and start drawing,
I close my eyes, head gleaming,
When I lie down I start dreaming,
One more thing I have to say,
'Why did I have to go to school today?'

Troy Stewart (9)
Stanford Primary School

Arsenal

A rsenal are the best, just can't test
R ubbish players should get sold
S enderos tackles players like Rooney
E ntering the pitch one hundred per cent
N o one in the League can better them
A mazing player, Adebayor bangs in goals
L azy teams always get beaten but Arsenal don't.

Rex Cobham (10)
Stanford Primary School

My Pet Monster

Me and my pet monster walked down the street
I saw my friends, they looked very frightened.
Sooo! Me and my pet monster skipped down the street
I saw my dog and she was whimpering
So then me and my pet monster walked back home
I went to the doorstep and he was gone!

Shaniya Robinson (9)
Stanford Primary School

Attention

Today my brother had his tonsils out,
He was very, very good, he did not scream nor shout,
But there is one problem, don't you see,
My parents have no time for me!
They watch over him - voices mild
Like he is their only child.
But I have to say loud and clear
I hope my parents are listening
My brother may be important, but I am another gem glistening.

William Radford (9)
Stanford Primary School

The Bad Things About Guinea Pigs

G uinea pigs are small but loud.
U ndersized they may seem, that's the way they get you.
I n a cage you put them but then they don't like you.
N ever nice
E ach guinea pig is different but they all plan to get out.
A little creature isn't just noise but pain as well.

P ick them up once a day so they may lay off you.
I ntelligent they may not seem but they will make lots of screams.
G uinea pigs are hyperactive but not too athletic.

Harry Victor Richards (9)
Stanford Primary School

Fun

Fun is as yellow as a bee in the sunshine.
Fun is laughter spreading through my friends.
Fun is bubbles in a bath.
Fun is as fast as a racing car.
Fun is the smell of cherries on a birthday cake.

Ryan Henningham (9)
Stanford Primary School

Ssh, Don't Wake The Baby!

Up the stairs,
Down the stairs,
Ssh, ssh, don't wake the baby!
Run to the kitchen
Need a drink.
Ssh, ssh, don't wake the baby!
Back upstairs to my bedroom,
Phew, close one!
Not a sound in sight,
But wait, a sound,
I forgot Teddy, left him in Baby's room.
Oh I have to be silent
Tiptoe to the room
Step on Ducky, *squeeeak,* whoops!
Baby sleeping.
Phew, got Teddy, back in bed.
Not a sound in sight,
But, wait a second,
I need the toilet
Silently I go to the bathroom
So far, so good.
I flush the toilet . . .
Ooooh! You woke the baby!
Whoopsy daisy.

Leyah Silvera (9)
Stanford Primary School

Love In The Air

L ove in the air
O nly for you
V alentine you are to me
E verlasting and true.

Naomi Carty (9)
Stanford Primary School

John Cena Rules

J ohn Cena is so great
O bjective complete, cannot be beat
H olds the championship every year
N ever beat, he is unstoppable.

C hampion and always will be
E dge is rubbish, John Cena's enemy
N ailed Nitro every year
A nd a great wrestler.

Sean Ebanks-Scully (9)
Stanford Primary School

Anger

Anger smells like the Devil is stabbing you with a fork,
Anger tastes like hot chilli sauce all over your lips,
Anger feels like you've been dropped in a burning rage of lava,
Anger feels like you have just been shot,
Anger reminds you of the Devil in charge of your brain,
Anger sounds like an aggressive song with violence,
                                    rudeness and swearing.

Jonathan Miller-Annor (9)
Stanford Primary School

Love

Love is the most beautiful feeling you could ever meet.
You drift away with love as a bird flying high in the sky.
Love tastes like the sweetness of fresh apples.
It smells like a rose, or perfume called Chanel.
Love looks like a red rose, fine and smooth.
It makes you feel unbelievably happy.
Sometimes love can stay forever with you and the other person.
Love is always produced in your heart.

Blazej Sroka (10)
Stanford Primary School

Love

Love sounds like pink kisses coming down to you.
It tastes like joy coming into your life.
It smells like a bakery in the morning.
It looks like strawberries with sweet sugar.
It feels like being tucked into your bed.
It reminds me of being hugged tight by my dad.
It moves inside your body like there's no anger anymore.

Remi Gyimah (9)
Stanford Primary School

Anger

Anger is like a fire but pitch-black with smoke.
Anger sounds like an angry bee buzzing around your ear.
Anger tastes like hot sauce burning through your veins.
Anger smells like red chillies rotting with fear.
Anger looks like racing cars colliding together.
Anger feels like you're being picked up by a tornado.
Anger reminds me of a sabre-toothed tiger growling through
a human heart.
Anger moves like a storm howling through the air.

Abdullah Ali (9)
Stanford Primary School

Love

Love is the colour of a red fluttering heart which glides
around the sky.
Love sounds like a young girl singing some lullabies.
Love tastes like red zinger hearts sinking into your mouth.
Love smells like roses spreading around my house.
Love looks like children sharing their joy outside.
Love feels like spreading nature and butterflies.
Love reminds me of my family and friends having so much fun.
Love moves like a papa bear playing with his son.

Kerith Minsende (9)
Stanford Primary School

Love

Love is as colourful as a rainbow reaching across the sky.
Love is butterflies slowly fluttering by.
Love is muffins with the glorious taste in my mouth.
Love is flowers growing around my house.
Love looks like families always getting along.
Love feels like children singing joyful songs.
Love reminds me of families giving gifts on Christmas Day.
Love moves like a monkey finding food for its children.

Rio Austin (10)
Stanford Primary School

Happiness

Happiness is like red hearts following you until you're old.
Happiness sounds like enjoyment with the children around.
Happiness tastes like lots of sweets melting inside your mouth.
Happiness smells like chocolate cakes cooking in an oven.
Happiness looks like a lot of smiles on your face.
Happiness feels like a bowl of strawberries.
Happiness reminds me of when I was in nursery and I was playing.
Happiness moves happily through the sky.

Neetasha Useree (9)
Stanford Primary School

Sadness

Sadness is a dark blue cat creeping around when I'm alone.
Sadness is an old lady crying for help.
Sadness is like a cold, cold ice cube freezing my heart.
Sadness smells ike soggy clothes hanging from a line.
Sadness looks like an upside-down smile hunting me down.
Sadness feels like a little cramp getting bigger and bigger.
Sadness reminds me of the last day I spoke to my gran
before she died.
Sadness moves really slowly to creep inside of me.

Annmarie Millington (9)
Stanford Primary School

Love

Love is like a token of peace to you and me,
So don't hold on to your sack of hate and stress,
'Cause when you're with that special someone it's the best.

Love is like a big red Care Bear
When you're on the Ferris wheel rolling in the air.

Love sounds like a nightingale singing at night
Don't go and look for it 'cause it's out of sight.

Love smells like Gucci perfume
I may assume.

Joshua Lessey (10)
Stanford Primary School

Darkness

Darkness is a fiery, misty colour.
Darkness sounds like cries from the underworld.
Darkness tastes like sweet and sour fried pig.
Darkness smells like burnt cow dung.
Darkness looks like an asteroid with dark, ghostly flames.
Darkness feels like a torture chamber.
Darkness reminds me of my biggest nightmare.
Darkness moves like a spider in the twinkling moonlight.

Chowhan Dookheea (9)
Stanford Primary School

The Mystery Singer

S he sings with a passion
I n everything she does
N ever will she give up
G reatness comes from the heart she says
E veryone can be a star
R iches do not matter, it's how you are inside.

Rachael Dowdall (9)
Stanford Primary School

My Dream

To dance is my dream,
Hard it may seem.
How I love to groove
And prove I can move.

As the time comes nearer to do my bit,
There's a nervousness I just can't admit.
But I do it quite fine,
The audience don't decline.

Fame gives me good fortune and wealth,
So I can help those who suffer bad health.
To make the world a better place
But also everyone will know my face!

Zoe Clark (10)
The Priory CE Primary School

Wonderful Island Of Dream

We found a mat,
A big bright mat,
We sat on it, the wind was blowing hard,
It lifted the mat with just me on it.
It sent me on to an island,
A wonderful island,
A shining island.
It seemed the whole island was sparkling with laughter,
A mermaid,
A unicorn,
A pirate.
Then suddenly it vanished into darkness
And I woke up.

Fuyuki Kuwabara (9)
The Priory CE Primary School

Goodbye

As we live our lives with love and joy,
We need to think about the people high in the sky.
Think about them even though they're not there,
Let them know that we really care.

Make a space in your heart for those who have to depart,
When you're sad and you want them there,
You know they're right over there.
They care about us up high,
They care about us down low
All you need to do is know . . .

Those who have departed and those who have to depart,
Are always with us in our hearts.
Let them know that you are there,
Let them know that you really care.
Make way for those to come
You know there is always one.
If I count to three then I will see
The dead in front of me.

Gemela DeSouza (10)
The Priory CE Primary School

A Fish's Body

As scaly as snakeskin,
As slippery as soap,
As shiny as a diamond,
As elegant as a dolphin,
As quick as lightning,
And how a flick of his tail
Makes him move.
How far, I just don't know!

Veda Clemson (8)
The Priory CE Primary School

Truffle

Truffle is my dog and I love him to bits,
His legs go out like a frog when he sits.

Truffle is my dog and he makes me laugh,
His fur is as warm as my winter scarf.

Truffle is my dog, he has a wet shiny nose,
He chases the squirrels up trees when it snows.

Truffle is my dog and he is my friend,
And he will stay with me until the world's end.

Natalie Brown (9)
The Priory CE Primary School

My Brother In Space

My brother wants to go to space.
I don't know why, as I look at his face.
It seems to be me he wants to be alone.
There's nothing to do on the moon but throw stones.
He acts like a clown with an audience around.
At least in space no one would hear a sound.
Up there in the middle of nowhere
If you needed the loo you would have to poo in mid-air.

Sophie Graham (10)
The Priory CE Primary School

From A Bird's Eye

As I soar through the sky I spy you below
The busy black ants crawl round the maze of their everyday life
I can see them scurry around on their flat grey ground
All I can hear is the cry of the morning
As it opens its eyes and wakes up the world
The uplifting wind flows through my feathers
I love the morning.

Rosie Tweedale (11)
The Priory CE Primary School

Mountains

As tall as the Eiffel Tower,
Like an elephant crossed with a giraffe,
So powerful.
You climb to the top,
Natural air blows against your pale face.
At the bottom, blooms of blood-red flowers,
Like the dabs of blood on leaves.
The leaves are as green as emeralds,
The mountains grow every year,
With crystal-white snow covering the tops.
The main mountain is made out of thick grey rocks,
As sharp as daggers.

Emilia Nuzzaci (8)
The Priory CE Primary School

My Cousin

My cousin is one and never leaves me alone,
She follows me around all day when I am at home.
She is as smiley as a puppy and as cheeky as a monkey,
She just loves to tease her mummy,
She also has a tickly tummy.

My cousin loves to play peek-a-boo,
When we talk about Grandad she says, 'Oh no!'
She loves to show her muscles and growls like a bear,
When she hears loud music she dances and swings her hair.
My cousin is noisy and sometimes screams real loud,
But I still love little her and when she smiles I feel proud.

Morgan Clark (9)
The Priory CE Primary School

My Little Monsters

They roll around on the ground safe and sound,
Covered in dirt all over their shirts
But Mum says it'll all wash out.
Always wriggling in the mud,
They don't think this play is dud.

They love to play fight with each other,
And when they see me, they run for cover -
Cos they lose against me,
I am their big sis you see!

I like it best when bath time comes,
The monsters get nice and clean.
Wrapped up all nice and warm under the covers,
I say, 'Goodnight. Sweet dreams.'
To my little brothers.

Chloe De-Smith (9)
The Priory CE Primary School

Speed

Speed is something that is really great,
No time to stop, wait or hesitate
But spare some time to listen to me
It won't take long, you will see.

When I'm going fast my heart beats faster,
I feel so good inside
And so alive.

Hayden, Rossi, Pedroser and West,
Motorcycle riding is what they do best.
Reikonen, Alonzo, and Hamilton too,
They probably liked speed when they were at school.

Red Walters (9)
The Priory CE Primary School

My Baby Brother

My baby brother is so cute,
But he's naughty too!

When he drinks milk,
He feels like pure silk.

When he sleeps,
He looks so sweet!

He'll always be next to me,
If he wants to hear a story.

He is so light
And his skin is so bright.

If he walks he will fall,
Because he is so small.

He is happy as a rabbit
And he has a cute habit.

He has tiny fingers and tiny toes
And he has bright baby eyes, cute baby nose.

He is attracted by the colour of baby-blue,
And he sticks to people like glue.

Jeremiah is his name,
When I call him, he smiles like we're
                    going to play a game.

Judie Jacob (8)
The Priory CE Primary School

Pigeon

I soar through the air as swift as can be,
Dodging the bombs as they rain down on me.
I go through the Underground and flying where I please,
After being used to fly overseas.

I do no damage but everyone hates me,
I have to look hard for every feed.
Bullets are always in my ears,
As they whistle past causing much grief.
I dive deep down among the leaves,
Looking for a safe haven for me to sleep.

A bomb is dropped near my face,
I'm sure these people aren't in the human race.
Killing each other without a thought,
Peace must surely be sought.

Thoughts rush through my mind,
What's happening? Where am I?
I can't see a thing, my vision has gone black
I am put in a sack and taken far, far away.

My message is taken off me,
My soul, my life, my reason to live.
This human has thrown it in the bin.
I can't believe my eyes,
What has happened to these guys?

Bethany Downey (10)
The Priory CE Primary School

Pigeon

I cut the air like knives cut bread.
I know no fear, I know no dread.
Only the wind in my ear,
The bullets seem to disappear.

No one fears my name,
Only the message I carry.
I have no fame,
Just the delivery.

Bullets come, bullets go,
Something happens, no one knows.
The blood is pouring over me,
I shall never reach my family.

Shooting down to the white cliff,
I can't even manage to lift.
My wings are damaged, my eyes aflame,
Still, I am lame.

Nothing to see, only blood,
Bones stick out like a masterpiece.
I love the peace, my head is a ball,
I have no fear as I start to fall.

Ben Slingsby (11)
The Priory CE Primary School

Spring

Hooray! Spring is here,
There are beautiful flowers everywhere.
I love the warm wind that blows through my hair,
Sometimes there's even a spring fair.

Hooray! Spring is here,
There are lots of green trees,
My mum buys lots of potatoes and peas,
But I hate the black and yellow-striped bees!

Dua Ali (9)
The Priory CE Primary School

Dizzy Dreams

A dormouse curled up, snoring in his sleep,
Dreams are for everyone.

Christmas pudding in the oven,
The smell of roast beef drifting out of the window,
Dreams are for everyone.

Fairies sipping honeydew whilst perched on tiny red toadstools,
Dreams are for everyone.

Fireflies lighting up a dark, damp room,
Dreams are for everyone.

Rabbits nestled in their burrows, ready for a midnight feast,
Dreams are for everyone.

You in your pyjamas dreaming,
Dreams are for everyone.

And they always will be!

Charlotte Hoskins (9)
The Priory CE Primary School

Young Writers Information

We hope you have enjoyed reading this book - and that you will continue to enjoy it in the coming years.

If you like reading and writing poetry drop us a line, or give us a call, and we'll send you a free information pack.

Alternatively if you would like to order further copies of this book or any of our other titles, then please give us a call or log onto our website at www.youngwriters.co.uk

Young Writers Information
Remus House
Coltsfoot Drive
Peterborough
PE2 9JX

(01733) 890066